July 197_

To Bob & Betty

With many thanks for your
kindness. We had a wonderful
holiday. God bless you both.

Janette & Cyril

WERNER FORMAN'S

NEW ZEALAND

WERNER FORMAN'S
NEW ZEALAND

Introduction & captions to the photographs by C. K. Stead

Captions for pages 1–7

HALF-TITLE PAGE: Figure in a landscape. See text p.15 for the facts about this unusual photograph.

TITLE PAGE: For facts about this scene, see the caption for p192. For the impact this otherworldly landscape made on Forman it is worth quoting from notes he made soon after taking the photograph; "The hub of the wheel of time. Two million years created tiers of sundials, moondials, stardials. Light and dark record the azimuth of heavenly bodies, a universe in motion around this *axis mundi.*"

THIS PAGE: Snow scene from the air, Southern Alps. Forman's notes, made shortly after taking the picture, refer to snow "clinging to and sliding off near-perpendicular slopes" and comment on the latent "power of fragile, weightless flakes", each perfect in itself, which, compacted into great glacial rivers, could mould and create a landscape, including those so-called "badlands" shown on the preceding page.

OVERLEAF: Spirits Bay, Cape Reinga, at the northernmost tip of the North Island where, according to one version of the legend, the explorer Kupe landed one thousand years ago. The spirits of the dead are said to depart from Cape Reinga, perhaps to return to the ancient homeland, Hawaiki.

Acknowledgements

Werner Forman would like to acknowledge the help of the following museums and collections in permitting the photography shown on the pages listed: Auckland Institute and Museum, Auckland, 64, 118, 119, 121, 127; Canterbury Museum, Christchurch, 158; Lance Entwistle, 53, 105, 221; Te Awamutu District Museum, 37; Hocken Library, University of Otago, 206; Okains Bay Maori and Pioneer Museum, 152, 222 (bottom); Museum für Völkerkunde, Abteilung Südsee, Berlin, 113; Museum of Mankind, London, 57 (left), 69; Museum of New Zealand, Wellington, 40 (top and bottom), 52, 54, 108, 115, 126 (left and right), 132, 135, 137, 138, 156, 157, 160; Otago Museum, Dunedin, 80, 207, 222 (top); private collection, New York, 57; Taranaki Museum, New Plymouth, 142.

Werner Forman would also like to thank the following museum directors, curators and collectors for their assistance at the time the photographs were taken, or subsequently: Dimitri Anson, Dunedin; Richard Cassel, Dunedin; Maura White, Dunedin; Virginia Stead, Dunedin; Roger Fyfe, New Plymouth; Jill Hamel, Dunedin; F. C. Hunwick, Te Awamutu; Gerd Koch, Berlin; Ron Lambert, New Plymouth; Anne Facer, Dunedin; Graeme Leitch, London; B. McFadgen, Wellington; R. B. O'Rourke, Wellington; G. S. Park, Auckland; David Simmons, Auckland; Dorota Starzecka, London; M. Thacker, Okains Bay; Michael M. Trotter, Christchurch; John C. Wilson, Christchurch; John C. Yaldwyn, Wellington.

First published in Great Britain 1994 by Harvill
an imprint of HarperCollins*Publishers*

This edition published in New Zealand 1994 by
Whitcoulls Limited, Private Bag 92098, Auckland

Photographs and preface © Werner Forman 1994
Text and captions © C. K. Stead 1994

ISBN 0 909022 17 8

Colour origination by Colourscan, Singapore
Printed and bound by C. S. Graphics, Singapore

Something, whose truth convinc'd at sight we find,
That gives us back the image of our mind

ALEXANDER POPE
Essay on Criticism

Giving back found images of the mind to T. and M.

W.F.

It's an awkward task to preface this book. You the reader can distance yourself from my dilemma by turning at once to the pages that follow. There a New Zealand novelist, poet and critic pre-empts in a straightforward manner most of what I could never have rendered as fluently. That leaves me with some of the more elusive consequences of a photographer's *wanderlust*, enforced and otherwise, and the matter of how some pictorial ephemera initially never intended for publication triggered a publisher's determination to bring the present book to life. Other related issues, for example, the persistent hold the islands exercise over many who come to know them, are even less easily put into words. I do not want you to take my word for it – instead of the word I offer the image.

> *No country upon earth can appear with a more rugged*
> *and barren aspect than this doth.*

JAMES COOK CONTEMPLATING THE SOUTHERN ALPS, 1770

I disembarked in New Zealand in the autumn of 1968. At that time I was working on a series of books named "With the Eyes of the Explorer" and after publication of *Marco Polo* James Cook was scheduled as the next subject. To see New Zealand *with the eyes of the explorer* I had timed myself to the season of Cook's arrival 200 years earlier. New Zealand's springs

and autumns can be rough and stormy. Cook complained during much of his six months stay of foul weather. I had come in the same season and got what I had asked for, and sympathized with Cook. Still, neither weather nor Cook's peculiar fish-eye view, taking in mainly coastlines and little else beyond, would have prompted me to forego a closer look at the islands. More compelling circumstances prevented me from lingering in New Zealand or anywhere else.

I was born in Prague and my roots are there. In spite of the increasing difficulties of leading an independent life in a totalitarian regime, it remained my working base until 1968, when the bonds holding me there loosened. By August of that year a short-lived, miraculous spell known as the Prague Spring came overnight to a rude end. To stay or not to stay was the question. The Golden City, as Prague was known, had become a frying pan. I turned my back on it and became a pariah zig-zagging around immigration authorities who would sooner dispatch an unwanted person back to the frying pan than grant entry or even passage. And back there I was wanted – for a five years stretch – one more dead albatross hung round my neck. Little did I know then that after 13 years of peregrination this spectre and a few more of the same feather would dissolve on the shores of New Zealand, that the first fully recognized international

travel document I ever held would bear the stamp: ISSUE OCTOBER 1981, WELLINGTON, NEW ZEALAND.

But that was to come, first I have to disown the persistent "blurb" tradition that setting foot in New Zealand was a matter of love at first sight. Instead, I arrived, did what I had to do and anon I left without a backward glance, bound on a convoluted route to Europe. Years of precarious travel and work followed. A dim, gnawing feeling that I had left in remote New Zealand something unfinished grew stronger until it surfaced as a book project, making a return to the islands mandatory – *The Maori: Heirs of Tane*, in pre-and early-contact times. Again there would be limits, a specific focus. Off-limits was the concrete-covered world of the Pakeha, and so too were his cattle, sheep and green grass. I don't need to tell a New Zealander that these are formidable limitations. But against my better judgment, mesmerized by the beauty of the country, I got sidetracked more than once.

Later in London, with all the films processed and more than 4,000 frames slotted into batches according to subject matter, I was left with a residue of a few images belonging neither here nor there. I took a long look, then stuffed them into a folder, and this became a file in need of a name. *Ephemera? Indulgences?* No, I scribbled instead across the cover:

No country upon earth can appear with more grandiose and subtle aspects than this doth.

W. F. CONTEMPLATING MILFORD SOUND AND MT TARANAKI, 1978

and brought it along to a publisher I had worked with years before. Besides being a trusted friend of mine, this man is a reliable critic of independent judgment. He, too, took a long silent look, but then surprised me: "Make this into a full-length book. It will take ages; don't dilly-dally around, goddamit, get cracking!" I felt I had to argue, pointing to the unattainable utopia of a project based on chance, which was dependent on being in exactly the right spot at exactly the right moment every time, a co-ordination of time and space that could not be willed. Getting irritated, he sternly refused to listen. I did not see any virtue in provoking a heated argument, not with a rare friend, not if he is tall, lean, disgruntled and an ex-paratrooper. That at least was the way I rationalized my shutting up. In truth, I would have been disappointed and depressed had I made him listen to reason. I dearly wanted to go on with that crazy idea, I desperately wanted to return to New Zealand. Why? Maybe the image *is* the answer. If I am fortunate this will become apparent to the reader.

WERNER FORMAN, London, June 1994

The Treaty House at Waitangi. Originally, it was a four-roomed cottage prefabricated in Sydney in 1833 and sent across in numbered sections to be built in 1834 in the Bay of Islands for the British Government's official New Zealand Resident, James Busby. The house has been greatly extended and refurbished since that time. In January 1840 the Treaty of Waitangi was signed on the lawn in front of the house. By this treaty the Maori chiefs ceded sovereignty to the Crown and all Maori were granted full rights as British citizens. Later that year Busby travelled to Sydney leaving the author's great-great-grandfather, Mr John Flatt, C. M. S. Catechist, in residence, charging him to keep the hens out of the grape vines, and later complaining that he had not intended Mr Flatt to take over the whole house.

NEW ZEALAND IS THE NAME by which the world knows three islands in the South Pacific (the North Island, the South Island and Stewart Island) lying 2000 km east of Australia and 9000 west of South America, stretching 1500 km north-south from latitude 34 to latitude 48, and by the year 1990 home to 3.4 million people, about 10 per cent Maori. The name was bestowed by the first European discoverer, Abel Tasman, in 1642; and some New Zealanders, wishing to remove their sense of their homeland from its colonial past, prefer to call it Aotearoa, popularly thought to be the original Maori name and to mean Land of the Long White Cloud. In fact it means something like Land of the Long Daylight, and it seems likely that it is not of ancient origin but was first used after European settlement began. The name used on some early maps, and on the Maori text of the Treaty of Waitangi, Niu Tireni, is simply a Maori version of New Zealand – one of those strange Maorifications of English which the early missionaries encouraged with the idea of expanding the vocabulary of Maori to make it more adequate to the changing times. An earlier name, Te Ika a Maui, refers probably only to the North Island, and derives from one of the many legends of the heroic man-god Maui, who is said to have fished the country up out of the sea using for a hook the magical jawbone of his grandmother.

Did the pre-European Maori need a name for it at all? To them, what we now call New Zealand must have been the world, surrounded only by ocean, except that there was in their mythology a place they called Hawaiki, from which their ancestors were said to have come in a great fleet of canoes, so that each of the sub-tribes (*hapu*) was linked to a larger tribe (*iwi*) that took the name of one or another of those canoes. Although this was one of those simplifications by which an oral culture commits its past to memory, it contained the basic truth that there had been a migration from a distant homeland; and in this Maori and Pakeha (non-Maori) New Zealanders have had common ground. Our forebears all came over the sea from a faraway place which gathered about it a certain unreality, and consequently a certain magic. To the children of the early settlers Britain must have seemed almost as remote and mysterious as Hawaiki to the Maori, and similarly the source of legend. The sense of remoteness, of isolation, has thus been part of the collective New Zealand psyche, producing in both Maori and Pakeha a deep attachment to the land, and at the same time an ambiguous attitude, both longing and resistant, to the larger world beyond the seas.

Werner Forman's New Zealand

Like every country in the world, New Zealand is subtly different in the mind of each person, inhabitant or visitor, who knows it. Each creates his or her New Zealand. Facts are important, and it is essential not to get them wrong; but they only take us so far. Beyond facts what matters is not opinion, but rather what the poet Yeats would call vision. There is no "correct" way to represent a country. As our title emphasizes, this book is not offered as yet one more attempt to mix all possible views and to extract from the porridge a broadly acceptable general picture. It is an image of a place and a society, and to some extent a history, through the eyes of one intelligent, sensitive, talented observer – Werner Forman – each of whose photographs is in effect a statement in the first person.

My accompanying text will also be in the first person. It will not attempt to repeat in words what cannot be said better than by the photographs. Rather, it will supply some facts beyond the photographs, and give at least something of my own view – that of a person for whom New Zealand is home. I will be offering a parallel commentary which should at times confirm, at others qualify, at others again possibly challenge, the cumulative impression of the photographs. But the photographs are the book's *raison d'être*; and because that is so the reader should know something of the photographer.

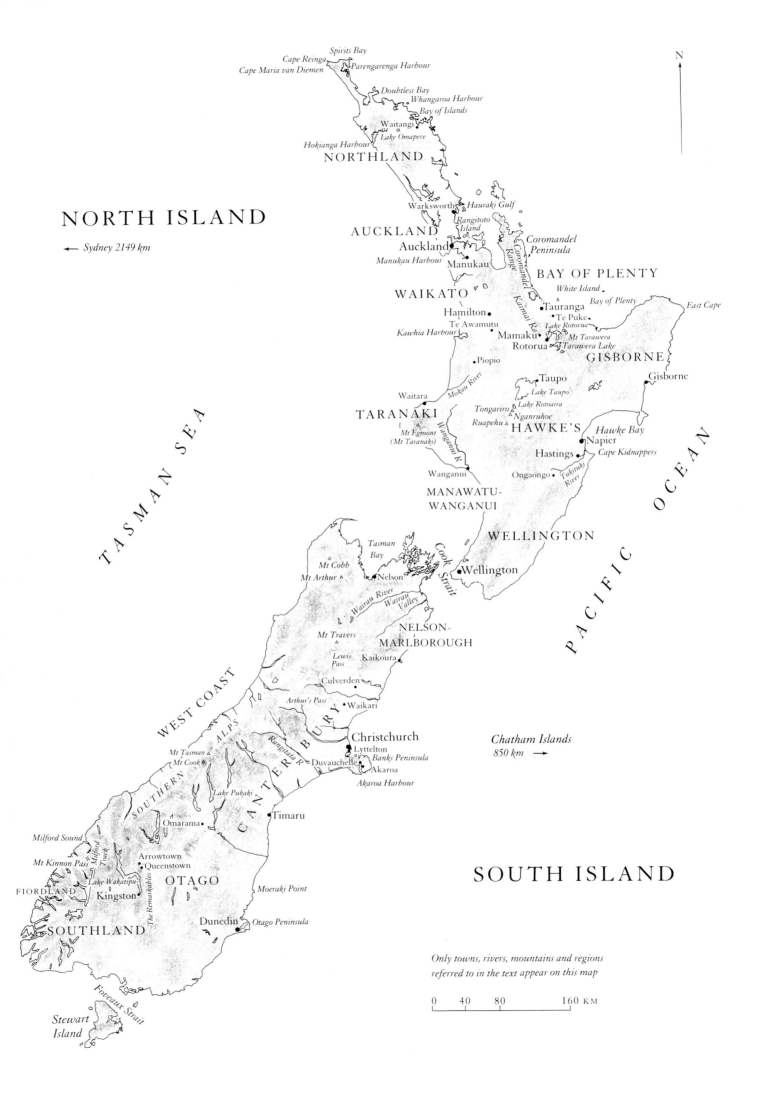

N

NORTH ISLAND

← *Sydney 2149 km*

Spirits Bay
Cape Reinga
Cape Maria van Diemen   *Parengarenga Harbour*

Doubtless Bay
Whangaroa Harbour
Bay of Islands
Waitangi
Lake Omapere
Hokianga Harbour

NORTHLAND

Warksworth   *Hauraki Gulf*

AUCKLAND
Rangitoto Island
Auckland   *Coromandel Peninsula*
Manukau Harbour   Manukau

WAIKATO   **BAY OF PLENTY**
White Island
Hamilton   Tauranga   *Bay of Plenty*   *East Cape*
Te Puke
Te Awamutu   *Lake Rotorua*
Kawhia Harbour   Mamaku   *Mt Tarawera*
Rotorua   *Tarawera Lake*
Piopio   **GISBORNE**
Gisborne
Taupo
Waitara   *Mokau River*   *Lake Taupo*
Tongariro   *Lake Rotoaira*
TARANAKI   *Nganruhoe*
Ruapehu   **HAWKE'S**
Mt Egmont   *Hawke Bay*
(Mt Taranaki)   Napier
Hastings   *Cape Kidnappers*
Wanganui   Ongaongo   *Tukituki River*
MANAWATU-
WANGANUI
WELLINGTON
Wellington

Karmai Ro.
Coromandel Range
Wanganui R.

TASMAN SEA

Tasman Bay
Mt Cobb   Nelson
Mt Arthur
Wairau River
Wairau Valley
NELSON-
Mt Travers   **MARLBOROUGH**
Lewis Pass   Kaikoura

Cook Strait

WEST COAST
Culverden
Arthur's Pass   Waikari

SOUTHERN   **Christchurch**
ALPS   Lyttelton
Banks Peninsula
Duvauchelle
Mt Tasman   Akaroa
Mt Cook   *Akaroa Harbour*

C A N T E R B U R Y
Rangitata R.

Chatham Islands
850 km →

PACIFIC OCEAN

Lake Pukaki
Omarama   Timaru

Milford Sound
Mt Kinnon Pass   *Milford Track*   Arrowtown
Queenstown
FIORDLAND   *Lake Wakatipu*   **OTAGO**   *Moeraki Point*
Kingston   *The Remarkables*

SOUTH ISLAND

SOUTHLAND   Dunedin   *Otago Peninsula*

Only towns, rivers, mountains and regions
referred to in the text appear on this map

Foveaux Strait

Stewart Island

0   40   80   160 KM

Werner Forman

Werner Forman was born in Prague in 1921. His mother was of a Jewish, his father of a Catholic, family, though neither practised the family religion. Forman's forebears were Czech, Polish, Hungarian and German, but his family thought of themselves as Czechs. This mixture of antecedents gave him a certain detachment. Asked about where his personal loyalties lie he is wary, explaining that "the rope of 'Vaterland' patriotism too easily becomes a noose", and that the spectre of those who have been caught in it is very real to him. But Bohemia, and above all the city of Prague, shaped his identity, provided bonds which deportations, incarcerations and prolonged exiles have only strengthened. Prague is his starting point, from which he sees everything else.

Forman describes his family as educated but poor, remembers his and his older brother's childhood as very happy, but acknowledges that it was restricted in terms of comforts. Aged ten he acquired a box camera. Around the age of twelve or thirteen he became obsessed with aeroplanes and began to photograph them. At fourteen – the minimum age for it – young Werner asked to be permitted to leave school. His parents discouraged this, and insisted that if he was to leave he must at least get himself qualified for some kind of work. He said he would like to be a pilot; and when this did not seem possible he elected photography, thinking that he would photograph aeroplanes. So he began his training. It lasted only six weeks, at the end of which time he had sold his first photograph – of an aeroplane. By the end of 1937 he was already official photographer to C.S.A., the Czechoslovak State Airline. But the German occupation of Prague in March 1939, followed by the outbreak of full war in September, cancelled for more than six years any thought of the future; and for Forman, as for many Europeans, life became a matter of survival. When, early in 1942, he got in touch with an underground organization in the hope that they would locate a death camp inmate for him and establish contact with her, he knew that he was asking a lot. In return, he offered his photographic skill, an offer which was accepted and which soon involved him in some of the riskiest photographic missions imaginable. Later that summer the Gestapo discovered the group's existence and rounded up all 80 members (only one of whom survived the war). Forman believed that even as an outsider he was in danger and thought it prudent to disappear, preferably without trace. The story of how he achieved this is worth telling.

Every Saturday young Czechs drafted for forced labour in Germany were farewelled at the Prague railway station by families and loved ones. Anyone could get into the station; but if you were young and male you could not get out. It was no use protesting that you were not one of those drafted, or that you had forgotten your papers – the story would not be believed. It would be thought that you had lost your nerve and were trying to escape. So Forman went to the station. When he was told to board the train he protested and said he had no papers. He was told he would be given temporary ones. He gave a false name, and by that means was shipped to Munich with a new identity. There he worked for two years until scarlet fever almost killed him, and rendered him unfit for work. He was given leave to return to Prague. As it happened the minister who had responsibility for the factory where Forman had worked was Goebbels. So now he had a pass in his false name rubber stamped with the name of the Reichsminister für Kultur, Dr Joseph Goebbels – a name to make any challenger quake!

By September 1944, his family, to whom he had returned, were under pressure because of the Aryan father's refusal to divorce his Jewish wife. They were sent to different camps – the mother, as a Jew, to an extermination camp in Bohemia (which by extraordinary luck she survived), the father as an Aryan Jewish-sympathizer, and the two brothers as Mischlings (mixed Jewish and Aryan) to camps in Poland.

But the Eastern Front was collapsing and the German army was in retreat. After four months the camp which held Werner Forman was abandoned by its guards. He set out with his father for Prague, a march of three or four days, wearing ragged clothes and wooden clogs, for much of the way dragging his father, who had a broken foot, on an improvised sledge through a ravaged winter landscape littered with frozen corpses, the night horizon constantly ablaze with gunfire.

Back in Prague, Forman was held in a detention centre. He volunteered to sweep the camp grounds – an unpopular job – and spent much time working around the gates, until he had become a familiar sight to the guards; but at the same time he was preparing a space wide enough for a thin person to creep through. When news reached him that a Gestapo poster had appeared in the town showing him as a wanted man, he knew it could only be a matter of hours before someone recognized and betrayed him. He made his escape at once, and survived the final months of the war only by keeping on the move, dependent on the goodwill and bravery of people who risked their lives to let him stay a night, and then he would be off again before daylight.

To have surfaced after six years of Nazi rule and war, Forman says, was like a sudden decompression that left him stunned, feeling neither elation nor joy, the stench of the death-camps literally still in his nostrils. He was reunited with his brother Bedrich, and as they began to recover from the trauma each became possessed by what he now calls "pipe dreams". Both worked on new technologies – Werner on experiments in sound and image in 3-D; Bedrich on the famous "Laterna Magica" developed by the Prague playwright and director Alfred Radok.

In 1947 the brothers began as a team to produce books on international art subjects which had not been written about in the Czech language. A year later the February Revolution, really a staged takeover by Moscow, establishing a hardline Stalinist regime, meant that the private publishing firms for which they had been working were closed down.

Their first big (and enduring) success came with a book on Chinese art, which was also published in London, and subsequently translated into 16 languages, ultimately selling 750,000 copies. The success of this book was typical of the many ironies and contradictions that make up Werner Forman's life. In the West, probably because it came from a State publishing house from behind the Iron Curtain at the height of the Cold War, the book was denounced by the *Guardian*, by Radio Free Europe and by the British Information Service as Communist propaganda; but in Czecholsovakia the Forman brothers were criticized by hardliners because their text made no ritual obeisances to Lenin and Stalin, and because the pictorial material included no portraiture of Mao and no "revolutionary art".

But this book was the most important single event in determining the future course of the Forman brothers' lives. They were now known to the international publishing industry as the authors of an art book which had had an unprecedented commercial success. Their work was sought after, Werner acting always as the photographer, Bedrich as the designer, and an appropriate writer of their choice doing the text. Their books were widely published and won important awards. Forman was continuing to experiment in his photography, attempting to capture a more real sense of three dimensional space, the key to which he felt was to be found especially in an awareness of shadows. Shadows, he was discovering, had a life of their own apart from the surfaces on which they fell. Forty years on, this fact is better-known, though still not fully understood; but at the time he felt that he was going through the known barriers of photography.

Forman's biggest problem, working out of a Communist country, was travel. Both sides of the Iron Curtain made life difficult for him. It was never certain that permission to leave would be granted; and once that had been obtained, there were endless obstacles in the way of getting visas. Often he departed without the necessary travel documents, and simply begged, bullied or cajoled his way through. But one way or another the books were done and published. Most were successful, many reprinted.

By the late '60s his ties to Prague had loosened. He still worked for the Czech publishing house, Artia, but he had commissions also from London and Vienna. His parents had died. The "Prague Spring" had been suppressed by Russian tanks, to be followed by what Forman calls the "Prague Winter". Now it was more than ever difficult to travel on a Czech passport, and conditions at home put an end to his hopes that he might remain a photographer of international subjects working out of Prague. He married a young American woman, left the country legally, but did not return when his exit permit expired and as a result became an exile, sentenced to five years jail which he would have served if he had returned. Yet he had no established right to be anywhere else.

For many years he kept himself one step ahead of various immigration authorities, surviving on short-term visas. It was not until 1981 that he got full British citizenship. It was also the year when, after a 13-year exile, he was once again able to visit Prague in safety. London is now his home, and the Werner Forman Archive, which publishers, museums and art galleries from every part of the world call upon for photographs of ethnic art and culture, is established there. But Forman is on the move nine or ten months of the year. His London-born daughter, Jofka, lives with his former wife in New York. His brother Bedrich, who remained in Prague, died recently. Forman's work is anywhere and everywhere.

To go back: it was a commission to do a book on James Cook that brought Werner Forman to New Zealand for the first time. That was in 1968, and since then he has returned again and again. The present book thus represents photographs taken over a period of more than 20 years. In part the special interest he developed – consistent with the work he had done elsewhere in the world – was in pre-European Maori culture and art. But it was not that interest alone which drew him back. There was something he wanted to capture which to his eye was unique. It was partly a landscape; but for Forman that means also a skyscape – and in New Zealand, grand and rich as the land forms can be, there is a vastness and variety of sky colours and cloud forms that frequently predominate over even the most imposing of mountains, plains, rivers and lakes. These skies are effects of light consequent upon the shifting airs through which it passes from moment to moment; and effects of light are also effects of darkness – those shadows Forman has learned to think of as three-dimensional. Often in his photographs (see for example pp 116–17) there will be brilliant light in the foreground and again in the distance, while a huge cloud-shadow lying across the middle distance will give the picture, properly reproduced, the sense almost of a hologram.

This impressive landscape which Forman began to photograph first in the late '60s was partly unchanged by human habitation. But much of it – the pastoral land, for example – though sparsely populated, had been transformed by European settlement; and there was again in that settlement something which took Forman's imagination and seemed to him a challenge to his skill as a photographer. What gripped him, and brought him back, was his sense that while the rest of the world was making itself international and consequently anonymous, removing itself from direct contact with the natural world, there was still in New Zealand a strong sense of, and feeling for, something belonging uniquely to the land forms and the sea presence – what Allen Curnow long ago called "the regional thing, the real thing". Wood and corrugated iron – those basic materials of our colonial buildings – interested Forman more than concrete and mirror glass; and he was fascinated by the way our early houses and public buildings seemed, often, not to have been built to show off the designers' skill, but to have grown according to need, making the simple best of whatever was available.

During the period that Forman has been taking these photographs many old buildings have been knocked over and replaced by big city developments. Internationalism, though late, has come to our shores. Some interesting examples of it will be found here. But Forman sees this book in part as a work of nostalgia – a record of, and an act of piety towards, a New Zealand that is vanishing.

Of Skies and What Lies under Them

After 40 years away from home the Australian writer Christina Stead returned in 1969, and was struck most forcibly by the southern skies: "Under the soft spotted skies of the North Sea I had forgotten the Australian splendour, the marvellous light . . . Everything was like ringing and bright fire and all sharpness."

When I first looked at some of Forman's New Zealand photographs in the office of our London publisher I recalled a very different collection of photographs of New Zealand I had been shown many years before with the idea that I might write an accompanying text. They were remarkable in their own way; but I had asked the question "Where is the sky?" It was if the photographer had gone about with her camera tilted a little towards the earth. In Forman's photographs the New Zealand sky – its many skies – contributes to that sense of space, of emptiness, of openness and opportunity, which visitors accustomed to enclosures of every kind find exhilarating or disconcerting. But a photographer's "subject", like a writer's, is only half the story. The other half is the person who is patient and persistent in waiting for visual phenomena, occurences, effects of light and shadow which will accord with his vision; and a master at getting them on to film. In that London office I was struck by the fact that Forman's skies, though always vivid, were often close to monochromes, as if a painter had chosen to work at one time in blues and blacks (see pp 6–7), at another in reds and orange, at another in yellow and gold (p 178). Some of them reminded me of landscapes by Turner, an artist I later discovered Forman greatly admires, because in them he sees something seldom caught in photography – a sense of sky in motion.

Skies in Forman's photographs are magical and they are symbolic. They threaten, they drift, they console, they invite, they forbid. They set limits and are limitless. They are never static. They reach away beyond what we know into what we do not and can never understand. They are Pre-Raphaelite and Post-Modern, Pakeha and Maori. They are aggregations and aggravations of colour, often violent, sometimes delicate. They are a universal irony, an expression of our human fate, and we in the southern oceans are different from the rest of the world only in having the best seats in the grandstand. It is strange but it seems right that a man whose life has been so buffeted by the cross-currents of European history should have travelled so far, and returned so often, to put on record what can be read, I think, as the symbols of his sense of our common lot, of our helplessness, and of our compensating sense of beauty and mystery.

Two examples will help to indicate the way in which this book has become a collaboration. During the process of making our selection Forman on two separate occasions put before me a pair of photographs of a building. One pair was of the old "wedding cake" tower of the University of Auckland; the other was of St Mary's Anglican Church in Timaru. Both buildings, which I suppose might be described as colonial Neo-Gothic, would have earned from Plato the special condemnation he reserved for those things which were not merely imitations of the Ideal, but imitations of imitations. Nevertheless, both have local significance.

In each case Forman put before me an impeccable and handsome representation of the building such as would gladden the heart of those who knew it and loved it; and beside that, a photograph in which the tower, though recognizable, is a shadowy form over which clouds in a very blue sky have arranged themselves with a symbolism so insistent it could never be excused except that the author was nature – or, if you prefer, accident. St Mary's tower (p 195) is encircled by a halo of bright, delicate, pure white and numinous cloud. The divine promise is so present in the natural environment, it quite forgives and puts into the shade our sins of architecture. And yet the promise itself seems too lightly made. The clouds are like visual laughter, gently mocking. In the University of Auckland photograph (p65) the white clouds sweep and surge up into the brilliant blue. Here is not a promise of the divine, but perhaps a Faustian one of knowledge and power. Again the man-made object is diminished by an accident of nature and rendered secondary to that promise; and again the promise itself seems lightly mocked.

It was up to me to choose – representation or symbolism – and Forman himself offered no interpretation nor expressed a preference; yet I was sure he was pleased that I showed not the least hesitation. In both cases I found symbolism, photographer's magic, the representation that goes beyond representation, irresistible.

A Shadow of his Former Self

Werner Forman is a slim, active, well-preserved man with a keen, slightly mournful face, always watchful, listening, not embarking on an opinion or an anecdote unless there is leisure to say in full what he has to say. His English, heavily accented, is somewhat formal, grammatically exact, drawing with precision on a wide vocabulary. He is wry and realistic about human behaviour, and his judgments always seem both charitable and wise. His patience in conversation, both in listening and in thinking out what he wishes to say, is an aspect of his character that goes into his photography.

Like the poets of the French Symbolist movement, Forman the photographer is in search of particular essences and states of feeling. To get what he wants he will wait for long periods in all kinds of weather, suffer all manner of discomforts, and if necessary return again and again to the same place. In that sense he is not just a recorder, but a creator of the images he publishes. *Werner Forman's New Zealand* is not simply a factual record;

it is also the imposition of one man's vision on the facts.

There are many anecdotes that might be offered about Werner Forman. One will have to do; and this one is chosen because it both illustrates his tenacity in pursuit of his goal, and has once again a kind of comic symbolism, especially in that it is unlikely that it could have happened anywhere else but New Zealand.

Forman likes subtleties of light that occur when the sun is low in the sky, either rising or setting, and with that in mind he set out some years ago, driving all night to a place where he was sure he would get a good view of early morning light on the slopes of Mt Egmont – or Taranaki, as it is known to the local Maori. He knew nothing of the New Zealand habit of jacking a wooden house off its foundations, lifting it on to a trailer, and carting it many miles by road to some place where the owner or a purchaser has a new use for it – an operation always completed in darkness in the early hours of the morning while the roads are empty. On this occasion two houses were being moved, preceded and followed by the necessary traffic officer escort and by a vehicle signalling that a wide load followed. Our photographer, however, must have turned into the road on which this convoy was travelling at a point that placed him between the two giant house-bearing truck-and-trailers.

In the darkness he saw something very large ahead of him and decided to overtake it, but there was a down-hill run, and whatever this giant was, it sped up as if unwilling to be passed. Now its lights picked up a bridge ahead. Forman decided to drop back, but as the truck moved to the centre of the road, in position to cross the bridge, the overhang of the trailer passed over his hire car, holding it so that he was carried forward. Either his car was going to be propelled straight into one of the bridge girders, or Forman had to get further under the trailer. Somehow, driving still at about 80 kmph he managed to tuck his car under the trailer and between the eight wheels ahead and the twelve behind.

Once clear of the bridge the truck moved left again into its proper lane. As Forman wrenched his car right to get unstuck and away from the roaring nightmare, the truck-driver must have seen headlights coming out from under his trailer. He braked – so violently that the trailer jack-knifed, and the house it was carrying began to break up. Timber showered around Forman's car, some of it penetrating end-to-end, through front and rear windscreens. Yet none of these shafts struck him. When the first traffic officer reached the scene, expecting to find a corpse, he discovered Werner Forman, pushed down into a tight ball under the crushed roof of his car, held there by pieces of timber, bruised and shaken, but otherwise unhurt. The timber was removed piece by piece, and the roof levered up. Forman got out, rescued his canvas bag, checked his camera and found it damaged but still useable. There was still time to fulfil the purpose of his night-long drive. While the traffic officers were engaged with the truck-and-trailer he climbed back into his car and with his head bent sideways under the still depressed roof, he drove on to his appointment with the mountain at sunrise.

One of the results can be seen in pp 140–141, where, as it happens, the early light on trees and water in the foreground is more remarkable than that on the mountain in the distance. But something else, unexpected and remarkable, came of this adventure. As Forman climbed to the position he had decided upon weeks earlier, the emerging sun cast the shadow of the hill he was climbing against the lower half of a stand of pines, making them look mysterious and subterranean, while the upper half of the trees stood out in bright sunlight. And as he moved to photograph this, his own shadow, clearly holding the camera, came up out of the shadowy half of the pines and was cast against the part in sunlight.

Werner Forman is reluctant to have his own photograph appear in this book; but I have insisted that that extraordinary picture (see half-title page) should be here, both as a reminder of his concern with shadows as well as light, and as an image of the man at work, still, and spectacularly that morning, a survivor.

In the Beginning

To a logical mind, unencumbered by any one particular faith, Maori chants which enact the Creation may seem less fraught with difficulty than the Christian account. Rather than beginning with a God who creates a Universe and remains its governor-in-principle and absentee landlord, the Universe in these chants comes into being out of nothing. In R. Taylor's 1855 translation the lines sound curiously like a lost poem by T. S. Eliot:

> From the conception the increase
> from the increase the thought
> from the thought the remembrance
> from the remembrance the consciousness
> from the consciousness the desire.

> From the nothing the begetting,
> from the nothing the increase,

> from the nothing the abundance,
> the power of increasing,
> the living breath.

Only when the Universe has had its beginning do the gods come into being; and thus, though powerful, they are closer to an image of mankind in being subject to powers beyond their own control. Rangi the sky father and Papa the earth mother are lovers clasped in an embrace which smothers the earth and deprives their children-gods of light and air. It is Tane, god of the forest, who drives them apart, lifting the sky father high into the heavens where he weeps at the separation. Now the earth becomes Te Ao Marama – the World of Light. To mitigate the pain they have caused their parents, the children-gods decorate their mother with trees and ferns, and their father with a cloak of stars. If we did not know what people had evolved this lyrical mythology, we would be sure that, unlike those for whom the Old Testament enshrined ancient wisdom and supernatural truths, they lived in a land of forests and ample rain.

Maui, the fisherman whose prize catch was the northern island of the country we call New Zealand, must have been a god, though mortal. He caught the sun in ropes that can still be seen at sundown, and (again with that jawbone of his grandmother which he also used as a fishhook) beat it until it promised to cross the sky more slowly, giving the world, or Aotearoa, its longer day. He also captured fire; and he might, by his bold assault on her sleeping form, have conquered Death in the person of the death-goddess, Hine-nui-te-po, ruler of the Underworld, had she not been woken by the laughter of the fantails that travelled with him, and closed her legs on him as he tried to enter her womb, crushing him to death (see p119, and caption).

But Kupe it seems was a man – like Tasman and Cook after him, a great sailor, navigator and explorer. He set sail from Hawaiki to find Te Ika a Maui, the Fish of Maui, and returned to tell where it lay and how it could be reached. With that information the great fleet of Maori myth was enabled later to set forth, and the new land was peopled. This simple and efficient history gave, and gives, any and every person of Maori blood an ancestry back to one or another of the canoes, and thus back to a single homeland peopled by gods and men.

That is one way – as good as any – of describing a beginning. Another, rather more prosaic, might be to say that the Maori are Polynesians (a race of great sailors and navigators) whose language and cultural connections with other Polynesians up through the Pacific are unmistakable. Archaeologists have concluded there were two distinct groupings of pre-European Polynesian inhabitants – the early Moa-hunters, or hunter-gatherers, who were here before AD 1000, and the later "Classic Maori", warrior-agriculturalists who wiped out and absorbed their unwarlike predecessors in the same way that, much later, Maori sailing from the mainland in a European vessel were to wipe out and absorb the peaceable Moriori of the Chatham Islands.

In appearance Maori seem to divide into two distinct types – one that looks as if it might be Asian in origin, the other notable for its hawk-nose (*ihu-kaka*, or *kaka*-beak) features, said to be characteristic of the Arawa tribes of the central North Island. But since it is thought that there are not, and have not been for several decades, any surviving Maori who do not have at least some non-Maori forebears, appearances are no safe guide to history or ethnic grouping. What we can say is that the "Classic Maori" who displaced and absorbed the hunter-gatherers, lived isolated on their islands for some (perhaps six or seven) hundreds of years between the time of their migration until that of the first European visitors – time enough to develop distinct, stable and integrated social, tribal and intertribal structures, codes of behaviour, arts and crafts, rituals and mythology.

There is a tendency now, equally among Maori and Pakeha, to romanticize that pre-European Maori life – to see it as pure and noble, simple and uncontaminated, carefree and natural. The ancient Maori is represented these days as a caring person, conservationist and deeply spiritual. No such romanticization is ever likely to be quite groundless; and the act of imagination required to enter into lives lived long ago and in close harmony with the natural environment is bound to promote it; but it should be understood that such a process merely imposes another alien and inappropriate value system on the image of an ancient race. It is, as one American anthropologist has recently pointed out, largely the invention of modern anthropologists and well-wishers. Though well-intentioned, it is a patronizing misrepresentation.

The Maori were a warrior race (Darwin, whose view seems to have been unfairly bleak, thought them the most aggressive people he had encountered anywhere), who lived by daring challenge and daring response, and killed or enslaved their tribal enemies without compunction. *Mana* (appropriately one of the few Maori words which has found its way into English beyond New Zealand shores) was something that had to be protected – both the *mana* of the individual and that of the tribe; and if *utu* (payment to compensate

for, or to avenge, a wrong) could not be exacted in any other way, then it was exacted in war – a war which in turn inevitably left debts of *utu* to be paid at some later time.

The Maori practised variously, and in varying degrees, cannibalism, slavery, infanticide and human sacrifice. In war prisoners were not taken unless they were wanted as slaves, or for later eating; and no distinctions were made between men, women and children, in the killing of enemies. The heart of the first-killed enemy in battle was often torn out and burned as an offering to the war god. After a notable opponent had been defeated and eaten the fact might be commemorated by naming places after parts of his body – his eyes in one place, his thigh-bone in another, his buttocks in a third. Theirs was a stone-age, oral culture, with all the limitations that implies in technology and in the complexity and detail of what could be carried forward from one generation to the next. They lived in fear not only of physical defeat but also of any breach of *tapu* (taboo), which might bring down nameless horrors on their heads. And at night the landscape was alive with *atua* – the spirits of the unassuaged dead who whistled among the grasses and out of the swamps, and might, in envy of the living, fall upon anyone venturing forth without a burning brand for protection. "Maori spirituality", in other words, like its Pakeha parallel, was at least as much a burden as a blessing; a form of bondage more often than a source of freedom.

As for being conservationists – the Maori, intentionally or otherwise, had burned off large tracts of forest and destroyed a number of bird species (including most notably the moa) before the first European despoiler ever set foot on these shores. Kimble Bent, a nineteenth-century European who lived as a Maori for a large part of his life and learned all their bush skills, records that one hunter could snare as many as three or four hundred birds of every kind in a single day. Even the white heron, often said to be sacred to the Maori, was snared and eaten; and the only bird safe from hunters was the morepork, *tapu* because his silent flight and "hundred eyes" declared him to be an *atua*.

All of which is insisted upon here not in order to score off ancient Maori ways, nor even to balance the books, but to make the point that modern intellectual concepts, and especially those which have (as they so frequently do) moral overtones, are no door to an understanding of pre-European New Zealand. One kind of moralist will condemn Maori barbarism, as if the Maori invented warfare and cruelty; another will sentimentalize a life which the sentimentalist would find insupportable. But to look passively, putting the mind into neutral gear, at Forman's photographs of pre-European Maori artefacts – the bone box, for example (p137), with its terrible brooding bird-like head and episcopal-seeming joined fingers, or the mysterious *toko wananga* (symbols of gods, p64), or "Uenuku", the incomparably beautiful carved post said to be the figure of a god (p37), is to find oneself responding to something at a level that transcends, or subverts, particular cultures. These are works of art which may have lost some of the meaning that belonged to their time and place of origin, but retain one that belongs to all times and all places. They are a point of imaginative entry, not only into the facts but much more importantly into the feeling, of life before European settlement began.

Another Beginning

Allen Curnow's poem commemorating the 300th anniversary of Abel Tasman's 1642 landfall, opens wonderfully with the sense of excitement, of almost infinite possibility, that the European exploration of the Pacific offered:

> Simply by sailing in a new direction
> You could enlarge the world.

But the second section looks, not through the sailors' eyes, but from the shore:

> Always to islanders danger
> Is what comes over the sea;

It is hard to think of anything which more vividly and immediately represents the inability of representatives of two cultures, each acting properly and with goodwill according to its own code, to understand one another, than those first shoreline encounters between Maori and European. The sailing ships with their masts and billowing canvas must have seemed impressive, and possibly threatening. But what was to be made of their pale-faced crews, dressed in strange garments and extraordinary colours, who when they had to bring a small boat ashore faced seaward rather than the way they were going? The only safe way to deal with them was to issue the traditional challenge, with all its fearsome warcries and threatening gestures. If the strangers responded correctly it would be clear they came in peace. The strangers of course, though they had usually been instructed to act with restraint and not use their

guns against poorly armed savages, responded as anyone does faced with what seems to be a threat to life. Neither side came off well in these encounters. Each had to learn at least something of the other's rules if more lives were not to be lost. Whalers and sealers, escaped convicts and men looking to trade, came ashore and were variously received. Mostly the European was welcome; where he was unwelcome he had no protection, and little chance of staying alive. Trade was soon established, and Christianity followed. Samuel Marsden preached the first sermon at the Bay of Islands on Christmas day 1814. In 1820 the northern chief Hongi Hika was taken to England where he met King George. "How do you do Mr King George", he said politely; to which the King replied, "How do you do Mr King Hongi," and showered him with gifts. These gifts Hongi exchanged in Sydney for guns; after which his tribe raged down the North Island, slaughtering their traditional enemies with unprecedented success. The Musket Wars had begun, and would continue for a number of years. Goodwill (and this is something which has happened often in the course of our history) had proved much more effective than enmity would have been in disrupting the established ecology of the Maori.

Not that anything of the kind had been intended. The settlement of New Zealand was significantly different from that of Australia. It was not a convict settlement. The Maori was considered to be a Noble Savage, unlike the Aboriginal whose appearance and way of life were so different they seemed to the eighteenth-century European mind primitive to the point of being sub-human. And finally New Zealand policy was strongly influenced by the missionaries and by London officials sensitive to the notion that indigenous people had rights, in particular land rights, which should not be disturbed.

Most of us grumble from time to time about "progress", and question what the word means; but its meaning is reasonably clear if it is used to designate those new things – especially technologies – which we could happily live without until we knew of their existence, after which we consider them indispensable. For the Maori, muskets became indispensable. So did gunpowder, bullets, cartridge boxes, blankets, fishhooks, nails, axes, adzes and hoes, iron pots, tobacco and pipes – and the list of necessities grew (and has gone on growing) with the years.

When we look at the goods offered in exchange for land, the bargains can be made to seem ludicrous – but that is because the land is now so valuable, and the goods, by the standard of our modern technology, relatively worthless. It should be remembered that if there were, as it seems, between one and two hundred thousand Maori, and if they were considered in some sense to have title to all of the land, then every Maori man, woman and child could be said to own roughly a square kilometre of it. Such a calculation is meaningless, except that it indicates how much land there was relative to land-users, and why, before the Crown put a brake on it by means of the Treaty of Waitangi, both Maori and Pakeha considered the barter of acres for implements and blankets a fair and reasonable trade. To the Maori of those years what was being offered was progress – something only individuals (and a very few of those) but never whole societies, refuse. The regrets were to come later. But one way or another Europe was going to reach into the South Pacific. It came first in the form of a relatively benign trade; but its consequences were damaging. Nothing in the islands of New Zealand could ever again be what it had been prior to the arrival of the European.

It is possible in imagination to project forward from the year 1800 several different futures for New Zealand; but given all the circumstances, and the history of colonization as it occurred, for example, in Central and South America, in southern Africa, and in the western United States, it is difficult to imagine one which would have been at the same time realizeable, and significantly better for the Maori than that which in fact occurred. And among the balance of forces determining the long-term outcome, perhaps the single most significant was the will of the Maori.

They were such a formidable military force they could, at any time up until 1850, have driven the Pakeha out of New Zealand, at least for a time; and even in the 1860s when some tribes did take up arms against colonial forces, and when the British military contribution seemed stretched to the limit, that might still have been possible if it had been the predominant Maori wish. But it never was. When it came at last to war, Maori fought with as well as against the colonial forces. In that sense the future of New Zealand was determined more by the balance of forces within Maoridom itself than by policy in London or by settler opinion.

Missionaries, Traders, Warriors

The Bay of Islands was the earliest centre of settlement, but soon missionaries and traders were scattered down the coast and in some inland places. In the 1820s, '30s and '40s they lived a strange life, surrounded by warring tribespeople whom the missionaries found eager to learn reading and writing but less interested, at least in the early years, in the Christian message which they were told required them to give up inter-tribal warfare and cannibalism. Sometimes, if the tribe a missionary or trader was associated with came under attack, he too could find himself in danger; but mostly he would be allowed to stand apart from local enmities and battles, which raged around him while he remained exempt from their consequences.

The missionaries relied, too, for protection, on Maori uncertainty about the strength of their particular *tapu*, and the power of their *mana* to call up support from beyond the sea. There are many stories of a Maori chief, enraged by some accidental damage to what he owned or (more likely) to his pride, confronting a lone missionary or trader whose only protection against instant death – a death which there was no effective power to prevent or avenge – was to stand his ground and give an impression of calm confidence in invisible forces at his back. In almost every one of these stories the lone Pakeha survives; and it must have been astonishing to those Maori who some decades later went to war against the colonists, to discover how often it was possible, and sometimes how easy, to win battles against them.

One early missionary records that there was a time when it was difficult in his area to travel any great distance without coming upon human remains. There is a story of a Bay of Plenty tribe, urged to give up cannibalism, who listened solemnly and next day turned up on the lawn of the mission house, unpacked baskets of human flesh, and proceeded to have a picnic. It is hardly likely that muskets had made warfare more common, but they had certainly made it more destructive; and this fact as much as any other must have accounted for the gradual success of the missionaries in persuading the tribes that the old warrior code could not continue. The rule was to be – if attacked, defend yourself; but no more warring expeditions simply for the sake of conquest or *utu*.

Missionaries and others who had regular contact during these early decades were consistent in reporting their high opinion of the Maori. A typical exchange before the Select Committee of the House of Lords charged in 1837 with reporting on the state of things in New Zealand goes as follows:

Q: Did you find the native Children easy to be taught?
Mr John Flatt: Very easy; very interesting; equal to European Children in point of Intellect.

The same witness, who understood and spoke Maori, reported that in the 1830s the tribes were eager to sell land, partly for what was offered, but partly also to secure a Pakeha presence in their area. And he spoke of their desire for the protection of the Crown against their tribal enemies.

It was with appeals of this kind partly in mind, together with a need to control settlement and the consequent purchases of land, and finally to forestall the French who were showing an interest in New Zealand, that the British Government sent out Captain William Hobson as Lieutenant-Governor in 1840 with instructions to draw up a treaty between the Crown and the native population.

The Treaty of Waitangi

6 February 1990 saw New Zealand officially commemorating 150 years of nationhood, dating it from the signing of the Treaty of Waitangi by Governor Hobson on behalf of the Crown and by local Maori chiefs on behalf of the native race. The treaty, it was said during these commemorations, was "our founding document". It was an example of enlightened colonization. It was seen as the reason why our race relations, though less than perfect, had been better than those of Africa, Australia, and the Americas.

On the other hand, it was said by some that the treaty had not been honoured. Argument continued over how it should be interpreted, and whether an exact interpretation mattered when so much water had passed under so many bridges. Some said it was the only legal and moral basis for the Pakeha presence in these islands – though it is most unlikely that many Pakeha, born here, descended from native-born New Zealanders, and with no legal status or citizenship anywhere else, were much impressed by that argument. There was a great deal of talk about present Maori grievances, and about the treaty as the basis for meeting them and resolving problems.

Werner Forman's photograph of the Treaty House (p 8) is taken from the lawn where Maori and Pakeha assembled in February 1840 to debate the treaty and finally to sign it. The wooden house is modest yet elegant, European in origin yet colonial in design and materials. Behind the cameraman's back the sun must just be rising over the Bay of Islands. Its light strikes full on the pillars and white front of the house. Pohutukawa trees shelter it on either side, and a flower garden is visible. At its back there is some blue sky, but a bank of heavy grey cloud leans over it, threatening. Will the sun disperse the cloud, or is the cloud closing in? It is a perfect image of ambiguous promise.

The Treaty of Waitangi was drawn up partly to authorize Britain's subsequent annexation of New Zealand. The signatories ceded sovereignty to the Crown, but retained their chiefly powers and the free undisturbed use of their lands, forests and fisheries. They were permitted to sell their lands, but for the time being only to the Crown, not direct to settlers. And they were granted full rights as British citizens.

The debate and the first signings occurred in February. By late May, while the document was still being hawked around the country receiving further signatures (for which the signer was usually granted a pair of blankets) Hobson was alarmed to hear that the New Zealand Company settlement at Port Nicholson (later Wellington) had appointed a magistrate without Crown authority, and seemed to be behaving like an independent state. He was also made anxious by information that the French were moving towards establishing a New Zealand colony. Feeling that he could not wait for further signatures, Hobson had documents prepared and declared New Zealand a possession of the Crown – the North Island ceded by the treaty, the South Island taken by right of discovery.

Historians have sometimes argued that if a majority of Maori chiefs had refused to accept the treaty put before them, Hobson could not have annexed the country. But the annexation of the South Island suggests otherwise. And since British settlement was going ahead with or without a treaty (in fact the most important purpose of annexation was to bring it under control) it might be argued that our early history would not have been significantly different if no treaty had been signed. The treaty was a formal convenience ("little more than a legal fiction" a Westminster Committee called it, while a New Zealand judgment of the 1870s declared it a "legal nullity") which was later to become, at least in the eyes of some, a formal inconvenience.

The Treaty of Waitangi illustrates very clearly how human beings use symbols, and what power they have. This homespun document, hastily cobbled together, inadequately translated for those who had to sign it, ambiguous and even contradictory in detail and consequently interpreted differently according to the interests of later interpreters, has become a focal point in our national debates, and its history has in some ways run parallel to the fortunes of the Maori race. At first it figured significantly. Then, as Maori declined in number and power relative to Europeans, the treaty receded in importance, except that it was often referred to as something legitimizing the power of the Crown. For a time the document itself was lost; and when recovered it was found to have been damaged by water and nibbled by rats. In recent years the increase in Maori population, the resurgence of interest in traditional Maori culture, and most importantly the influence of an international movement towards recognition of the rights of indigenous peoples, have combined to restore the treaty to prominence. "Honour the treaty" is now a popular slogan, though what this might mean in real terms is not always clear.

Often the spirit rather than the letter of the treaty is invoked, meaning, it may be supposed, that if the intentions toward the Maori race were honourable then the welfare of that race is a measure of how far it has been honoured. This is reasonable up to a point, except that it suggests the Crown (itself a symbol) and never forces beyond human control, nor the Maori themselves, must be held responsible for any and every Maori misfortune – a shift of moral emphasis which some may see as only another, though currently fashionable, form of paternalism.

A balance sheet, by this measure, would be difficult to draw up. The most contentious issue has been land. The treaty, at least in its English, though not in its Maori version, guaranteed Maori use of lands, forests and fisheries. In effect it gave the Maori race Crown title to every square centimetre of New Zealand, which at least one notable historian, William Pember Reeves, has suggested may have been a good deal more than the signatories would have claimed for themselves if they had been asked. One hundred and fifty years later, though Maori land is still extensive, most of New Zealand is owned by Pakeha or by the Crown.

However to confer title is to confer also the right to sell, so it might be argued that the treaty, despite good intentions by those in London who ordained it, was not altogether unlike the musket: it seemed to offer power and protection, but its potential for harm was as great as, or greater than, its potential for good.

The problem was settlement. It was proceeding apace at the time when the treaty was signed, encouraged by tribes who could not foresee its outcome. As more and more settlers arrived, the demand for land increased, and at the same time, gradually and inevitably, power slipped away from the Crown in London and passed to those on the spot. The British side was not united in its notion of what was a fair and just way to proceed. Policy-makers in London, who had nothing to lose, thought of the Maori, while the settlers, who had committed their all, thought of themselves and, more to the point, of their children.

Nor were the Maori united in what they wanted. They liked the profits land sales offered, and the trade a Pakeha presence brought to their region; but they soon began to see that if sales went on unchecked, they might be dispossessed as a race.

The treaty had said that Maori land could only be sold to the Crown. This meant, often, that "market forces" did not control prices, and the Crown sometimes bought cheap and sold dear to the settlers. There were periods when the Crown gave up its right to pre-emption; but this too led to abuses, particularly when chiefs sold without proper consultation with their tribe, or did not fairly distribute the profits of sales. Land courts were set up to deal with this kind of problem, but they were not always successful. When, in 1860, a question of the sale of land finally brought war, the occasion was a Maori offering for sale to the Crown a block of land at Waitara in Taranaki which he had no right to offer – an action he took only in revenge against a chief with whom he had quarrelled over a woman.

In the 1850s the Maori tribes of the central North Island tried seriously to come together and form a league which would check the loss of land and resist the pressure to sell which was being exerted by the settlers. In the Treaty of Waitangi the chiefs had the means by which they could have achieved their goal. But they were tribal people. For traditional enemies to act consistently in unison was difficult. The King Movement, as it was called, established some kind of centre for Maori nationalism; but one way or another sales continued. In the end it was left to the radicals to take the law into their own hands. War with the Pakeha meant win or lose. The tribes which chose that option seem, if our most recent historians are to be accepted, to have won the battles but lost the war.

Complaints about losses of Maori land frequently concentrate on confiscations which followed the wars of the 1860s. There is no doubt that in some cases these were unjust, even if in others it could be argued that the tribe in question, by going to war with the Crown, had abrogated the treaty and so could not logically claim its protection against subsequent punishment. But even supposing that all such confiscations were wrong, they amount in fact to a very small fraction of the land lost to Maori, by far the majority of which was sold. Sir Keith Sinclair records that by 1873, when the wars and consequent confiscations were over, Maori "still owned about three quarters of the North Island. They sold millions of acres over the next 30 years". There is no point in blaming settlers who bought land in good faith, whether from the Crown or direct from the Maori. But nor is there any point in blaming Maori for yielding to short-term profit. Partly the problem sprang from a European convention of individual ownership imposed upon a Polynesian one of collective use. Partly it was simply a consequence of a process which there was no one, not even the British Government, with the power or the understanding to control. Caught between the quick profit to be had from a sale and the long term conversion of land to the kind of farming use Europeans made of it, Maori most often sold, lived on the returns, and left it to a later generation to regret what had been lost – and in some cases try to reclaim it.

Ownership of land, then, which the Treaty of Waitangi was meant to render uncontentious, has been, and remains, a matter of bitter argument in New Zealand. In the matter of civil rights, by contrast, there is less ground for dispute. The treaty granted Maori full rights of British citizenship. Because Maori land was communally held Maori men were given universal suffrage in 1867 while Pakeha men had still to qualify by individual land ownership; and Maori women received the vote along with Pakeha women in 1893, the first in the world to gain this right. It was also in 1867 that four Maori seats were established so there would be Maori voices in the parliament; and for a very long time now, Maori have had the choice of voting either in their local electorate or in one of the four Maori electorates, which gives them an option not available to Pakeha to direct their vote where they feel it will be more effective.

Education, health care and social welfare have been and are available equally to all New Zealanders, irrespective of race; and if in recent years there have been some discriminations, these have been positive, reserving places in law schools, medical schools, teachers' colleges, and so on, for people of Maori descent even if their educational performance has been below that of Pakeha applicants.

These are indisputable facts; but many would argue that another set of facts tell a different story. Through the nineteenth century the Maori population declined so dramatically they were referred to as a dying race. It was neither warfare nor poverty that was destroying them, but European diseases against which they had no immunity. The only major disease Europeans could control during those years was smallpox, and as early as 1850 there was a programme for Maori vaccination. By 1859 it was estimated that two-thirds of the Maori population had been vaccinated. But there was nothing that could be done about "minor" illnesses like influenza and measles, which took them off in large numbers.

But at some point around the turn of the century, whether by intermarriage with Pakeha, or simply reduction to the strongest stock, the race developed the necessary resistance to such ailments, and the Maori population began to climb again. From that point on it ought to have been plain sailing; but that has not been the case. Though there have been, and increasingly there are, Maori

who are successful in our society and in the world, statistics show that Maori educational performance and health are poor compared to Pakeha, and that their rate of unemployment and of crime is high. These are the unpalatable facts which lie behind the slogans "Honour the Treaty" and "The Treaty is a Fraud", and prompt Maori radicals to argue for separate Maori development.

For most of the first half of the twentieth century Maori were almost invisible to New Zealand's city dwellers. In my Auckland suburb in the 1940s I can remember one or two elderly Maori women who wore the *moko* (tattoo) on their chin; and a few Maori children in our classrooms at school. Maori remained mostly in rural areas, usually close to their traditional tribal *marae* (forum).

During the Second World War the Maori Battalion generated great public interest and patriotism. It seemed to ordinary New Zealanders to symbolize good race relations at the same time that its heroic exploits in battle were a cause for pride. After the war Maori began to move into the cities, and particularly into Auckland, looking for work. They bought houses, cars, refrigerators, washing machines and began to become suburban people with the same middle-class aspirations as the rest of us. And in the following decades there was a steady inflow of migrants from the Pacific islands, so that the face of our northern cities changed. By the early 1970s the inner-city Auckland school my children attended was 60 per cent Polynesian.

People of Maori descent are now about 10 per cent of the population. Among them are doctors, lawyers, entrepreneurs – but for the moment that is a fact to be mentioned because it is new and statistically untypical. Starting from behind, and with the loss of that secure tribal centre and of its associated *mana* and confidence, many Maori have found the going tough in the towns.

One possible view of all this is that Pakeha history in its dealings with the Maori race has been one long effort at damage control – and inevitably only partially successful. There have been periods and pockets of anger, and times of violence. The fear of the settlers in remote parts of the country, particularly in places like Taranaki where harassment and massacres occurred in the 1860s, and the long residue of bad feeling after the danger had passed, should no more be overlooked as factors in our history than should the very deep resentments of Maori who have felt themselves dispossessed by a system of law and custom imposed by forces beyond their control. But there has been throughout these 150 years a consistent predominance of genuine goodwill between the races, and of realism on both sides. The Pakeha admiration for the Maori, though sometimes sentimental and unrealistic, has been genuinely felt. It is hard to see how a society which in the 1990s reveres and takes as its popular heroes Maori personalities as different as Dame Kiri Te Kananwa, Dame Whina Cooper, Sir Howard Morrison, Mr Winston Peters and the late Billy T. James, can be seen as racist.

Yet the problems remain, and the Treaty of Waitangi, honoured or ignored, makes little difference to them. The treaty is merely the symbol of our coming together, and of the consequences. The intractable fact remains that Maori, considered collectively, are still not doing as well as their Pakeha counterparts. Given the collective will that this should change, how is an improvement to be achieved? How really helpful is it to help people on the basis of their ethnic origin rather than on the basis of demonstrable need? Does turning a disproportionate number of Maori into visible dependants in our society make the problem better – or worse? Are Maori, especially the young, helped by an educational orthodoxy which encourages them to believe they have been wronged by history – or is that just another unintentional gift of poisoned chocolates?

Finally there is the question of integration. Fifty years ago it was considered, by both Maori and Pakeha leaders, that Governor Hobson's words as each chief signed the treaty, "He iwi tahi tatou" (Now we are all one people), was a proper aim and object of race relations in New Zealand. That is no longer the case. Ignoring the fact of how many national groups and races are represented in post-1840 immigration, Maori leaders prefer to say that we are one nation but two peoples. There has been in recent years something called "a Maori renaissance" – a reassertion of Maori identity and culture. The hope is to save that identity and culture from extinction, and to build confidence upon them.

There are many possible responses to this hope and to official policies consequent upon it. My own is to understand the motives and to wish them luck, while wondering whether something so conscious and deliberate can have a lasting effect. When you are working, and belatedly, against time, time usually wins. The sugar is melting in the cup. The flavour of the beverage is changed for ever, but the grains are no longer what they were. Once begun, this is a process that can't be put into reverse.

The Skin of the Fish

It may be that Maui was of a race of giants; or perhaps he and his brothers, like legendary figures from other cultures, grew in size as occasion demanded. Maui was the typical mythic hero, the youngest and despised of a large family of brothers. On their famous fishing expedition he was denied hooks, so he resorted to the old lady's jawbone. When he had hauled up from the sea what we now call the North Island his brothers at once began hacking into it with knives and other implements. The skin of the still-living creature wrinkled and shuddered – hence the rugged terrain of the island; and this story may also explain why the skin still at times moves.

In an animate universe such as the Maori occupied, everything has a personality and a story. When you fly from Auckland to Wellington you see Taranaki (Mt Egmont, 2518 m) to the right, almost directly below the aircraft, and to the left, Ruapehu (2797 m), Tongariro (1968 m) and Ngauruhoe (2291 m), all snow-capped, often pushing through cloud, Ngauruhoe with a feather of steam rising from its crater.

Taranaki once lived together with his brother mountains, but fell in love with Pihanga, wife of Tongariro, and was driven out, amid violent eruptions, for adultery. His path towards the coast carved out the Wanganui River; and the clouds and mists that are seen from time to time closing in on his summit signal the return of Taranaki's grief at the memory of his love and his loss.

Of course myths and mythic explanations overlap and are not always perfectly consistent one with another. One Maori legend has it that a great *tohunga* (chief), Ngatoro-i-Rangi, who came with the Great Fleet from Hawaiki, was the first explorer of the hinterland. When he came to the mountain region he climbed with his slave Ngauruhoe, not realizing, because he had never encountered it before, that one could die of the cold. Up in the snows, Ngatoro was so absorbed in the wonder of the place he failed to notice, until the cold began to affect him too, that his slave had frozen to death. Now, to save himself, he called upon the powers of his sisters in the homeland, Hawaiki, to send him their sacred fire. It came under the sea, bursting out first at White Island in the Bay of Plenty (still an active volcano), then in the thermal region around Rotorua, and finally up into the mountains, warming Ngatoro and saving his life.

Curnow's poem quoted on p 17 suggests that for islanders danger is what comes over the sea; but if geological time were not, compared to human time, slow motion, we might think that in our own case danger is what lies under our feet. Our largest lake, Taupo, in the central North Island, is one huge (1554 square kilometres) crater from an eruption larger than Krakatoa – so large it must have had the effect, over many hundreds of square kilometres, of an all-out nuclear attack.

The cities are not altogether safe locations either. Auckland is built on an isthmus dotted with hills like Mt Eden, One Tree Hill, Mt Albert, Remuera, Mt Hobson, Mt Victoria – thirty or more volcanic cones, each with its extinct crater and its surrounding scoria and cave landscape marking where moulten lava flowed down from the growing mound of hot porous volcanic rock. The most recently erupted of these, one of the landmarks by which Aucklanders identify themselves, is the island of Rangitoto (see pp68–9) in the Hauraki Gulf, its name, Bloody Sky, suggesting that Maori were present to see it erupt. Lake Pupuke on the North Shore, and the Orakei Basin on the town side, are both open craters probably from eruptions too sudden and violent to form a cone.

Wellington is built on a major fault line, subject to earthquakes from time to time, one of which, one day, is certain to be major in scale and possibly disastrous in effect, though modern building codes are designed to minimize damage of that kind.

In Rotorua and the surrounding countryside the crust is so thin and the strata so active underneath that mud pools at Whakarewarewa and Tikitere bubble like porridge, water boils in pools, geysers erupt, steam hovers over street drains and floats out of cracks in the ground (p100), and throughout the whole region there is the smell of sulphur. On pp102–3 we see steam rising from a hot lake and drifting up over cliffs in the distance.

Since European settlement began the worst eruption has been that of Tarawera in 1886, and the most damaging earthquake the one that struck Napier in 1931. The crater of Mount Tarawera, seen from the air in one of Forman's breathtaking aerial photographs (p101), reveals how the violence of the eruption actually split the mountain in two. An extraordinary record of the event was made by a young woman, Julia Maude Bennett, daughter of a sea-captain, who on the night of the eruption took a piece of cardboard and oil paints into the family garden at Te Puke, exactly 50 km from the mountain, and painted what she saw (p100). The light and dark of the sky and the silhouetted trees give the feeling of a peaceful night and a long view towards distant mountains; but there, dominating the whole scene, three separate and huge vents are exploding, violent and fiery red. It was an eruption that killed 153 people.

It was said that a chiefly *tohunga*, Tuhotu of Te Wairoa, had predicted a disaster. He was buried along with his village that disappeared under the showers of Tarawera's volcanic ash, but almost five days later local Maori, though reluctant, were persuaded to dig for him. He was found, still alive, and was taken to hospital where he warned that if his hair was cut he would die. It was, and he did – his powers of prediction had not been diminished. His hut with its carved lintel can be seen on p104 together with a rare example of a stone storehouse, also disinterred in what is now known to tourists as the Buried Village.

On the east coast the seaside town of Napier was destroyed by the earthquake of February 1931. What was not shaken down was burned in the fires that followed. In a small town a death toll of 256, together with the destruction of most major buildings, was an unimaginable disaster; but it had one curious and favourable outcome. The town was redesigned and quickly rebuilt under the direction of a talented and lively group of architects led by Louis Hay, all influenced by the most modern style of the time – Art Deco. It was a style which had its moment and then became unfashionable. By the 1960s Napier looked dated, and treated its buildings with indifference, as if they were part of the misfortune of 1931. Then in the 1980s Art Deco came back into fashion, with the result that Napier was all at once recognized as one of the world's most perfect and coherently built towns, given over almost entirely to a single style – an effect which makes it comparable, one British architect has suggested, to Bath. Page 129 shows the entrance to what was the Administration Building of the National Tobacco Company of 1935, considered to be Hay's masterpiece; while p128 shows typical interior Art Deco decoration in Napier's City Theatre.

Another example of the North Island's unpredictable surface is the Tangiwai disaster of Christmas eve 1953, when the crater lake which sat like a great holding tank at the summit of Ruapehu simply broke out and flooded watercourses below in a matter of minutes. Before anyone had registered what had happened a viaduct carrying a railway line was washed out just as the Wellington to Auckland night-express passed over. The express fell into the flooded river and 150 were killed.

That the Maori saw the North Island as Te Ika a Maui suggests they had some sense of its total shape as represented on a map. Stretching away to the south, larger, more stable, lay the island they sometimes referred to as Maui's *waka* (canoe), which is another way of suggesting what South Islanders mean when they refer to their island as the Mainland.

A line in one of Allen Curnow's poems likening the map of New Zealand to "a child's kite anchored in the indifferent blue" might more aptly describe the North Island – a kite flown by another of those outsize legendary heroes, his feet firmly planted somewhere among the Southern Alps.

North Island mountain climbers (of whom Sir Edmund Hillary, p71, is the most famous) begin learning their skills on the slopes of those central North Island mountains; but they have soon, if they are serious, to transfer to the Southern Alps, where peaks of over 2000m are commonplace, and where the highest, Mt Cook (photos on pp180–185), reaches 3764m.

South Islanders are rugged people. If the mythic view sees the North Island physically as slighter, added on, "offshore", that, I think, matches something in the post-1840 human character of each island. Not without some justification, South Islanders, though now distinctly in the minority, probably see themselves as representing the basic Pakeha New Zealander, rugged, dour, practical, reticent, to which in the North Island cities certain graces and pretensions have been added, like a coat of paint over weathered boards.

But if we are to talk of national character, and in particular of the human character of the different regions of New Zealand, we have to return to history.

The Four "City States"

The largest regions of pre-European Maori population were in the north and east of the North Island. Maori numbers remain high there; and the home *maraes* of very many city-dwelling Maoris are still in those areas.

The first significant European settlement was in the north – the Bay of Islands; but as 1840 approached the Wakefield family's New Zealand Company planned settlements in Port Nicholson (later Wellington), and along the west coast up to Taranaki. In fact Taranaki (Mt Egmont), rising from the plains with such classic symmetry to a fine, snow-covered pinnacle, is represented stylized to the point of idealization in an early (and very lovely) painting by Charles Heaphy, draughtsman and artist to the Company – a representation which seems to make the mountain a symbol of settler dreams and aspirations.

The Wakefields hoped, and confidently expected, that the capital of the new nation would be established at Port Nicholson. When Governor Hobson signed the Treaty of Waitangi and declared the Crown sole legitimate buyer of land, thus casting all of the Company's purchases in doubt, and followed this by announcing the capital would be Auckland on the Waitemata harbour, the Wakefields' alarm and anger were immense. Along with many individual settlers they felt they had been dispossessed.

In time a compromise was reached in the matter of the land purchased prior to the treaty; but the Wakefields continued to pour scorn on the treaty, suggesting (not without some foundation in truth) that signatures had been bought, that those who signed did not always have any real or significant authority, and that those who did have authority could not have understood the document because the missionary Maori into which it had been translated was barbarous and made an absurdity of the original English.

On the other hand the Company's purchases had been made in a most haphazard and perfunctory way, and were therefore certain to create conflict and discord. For example in 1843 at Wairau near Nelson, Captain Arthur Wakefield, attempting to survey land for which the Company title was extremely dubious, found his party opposed by Maori headed by the chiefs Te Rauparaha (who had recently come down from the North Island and conquered the area) and Te Rangihaeata. There was a brief foray in which the Wakefield party were defeated. Wakefield ordered his men to surrender, expecting British rules to apply, but the wife of Rangihaeata had been shot in the skirmish. *Utu* was demanded and the remaining Pakeha were executed in the usual Maori way – a blow to the head. Governor Fitzroy (successor to Hobson) decided that blame in the Wairau incident lay with the Company, and that no punitive action should be taken – a finding that must have been encouraged by the fact that no military force strong enough to take such an action existed in the new colony.

Auckland and Wellington were both established in 1840. In July of that year a ship from Britain arrived in Wellington harbour to discharge goods and passengers before sailing to Auckland carrying the new Government House which had been prefabricated in England on the model of the house built for Napoleon on St Helena. The Wellingtonians decided that the kit-set mansion should be hi-jacked, thinking that setting it up in Wellington might force the Governor to take up residence where they believed he rightly ought to be. The captain resisted this pre-emptive strike, however, and the Governor's house reached its proper destination.

The Wakefields were highly critical of the Waitemata location and of Governor Hobson, accusing him of incompetence, of taking too much notice of the northern missionaries, of failure to exercise his powers, of indecisiveness, and of enticing to Auckland artisans

Port Nicholson needed. Charles Heaphy, a good Company man, described the Auckland isthmus as a desolate place, strewn with volcanic rock of every size from pebbles to huge boulders and outcrops – a description which sounds improbable now, but which my own childhood memory of areas around Three Kings and Mt Roskill, still undeveloped in the 1940s, partly confirms. What Heaphy did not take into account was how those rocky areas could be landscaped, and how marvellously fertile the volcanic soil would prove to be, especially when gardened in a climate as consistently mild as Auckland's. While the hills around Wellington still look wind-swept and barren (which is their beauty and distinction), Auckland is a city in which gardens have burgeoned and where a continual effort is required to keep them under control.

All of this laid, right from the start, the foundations for animosity between the towns of Auckland and Wellington, which persists in some degree, surfacing from time to time in sporting rivalries, arguments about the weather (that Wellington is too windy, Auckland too humid), popular (mis)representations of each by the other (that Aucklanders are philistines obsessed with sailing and money, Wellingtonians weather-bound, boring bureaucrats), and literary feuds between the writers of each city.

It was probably the prosperity of Dunedin which brought about the 1865 shift of the capital to Wellington, the central city, which meant that the distance travelled by legislators from Auckland and Dunedin would be about equal. This gave new life to the Wellington settlement, its wealth, as with any capital, now coming largely in the form of taxation from around the country. But in this century Auckland has attracted the population, its 1990 count of 800,000 amounting to more than the combined totals of Wellington, Christchurch and Dunedin.

The southern cities got started a little later – Dunedin in 1848, Christchurch in 1850. In the early 1840s Edward Gibbon Wakefield had succeeded in interesting the Free Church of Scotland, a breakaway Presbyterian group, in establishing a colony of its own, and for this the site of Dunedin (first called New Edinburgh) had been chosen, and land bought from the local Ngai-Tahu tribe.

1848 brought the first two ships, the *John Wickliffe* and the *Philip Laing*, with a complement of settlers led by Captain William Cargill and the Rev. Thomas Burns. Also travelling on the *John Wickliffe*, though intending to move north to Port Nicholson, was Thomas Arnold the younger, brother of Matthew Arnold. Since the Rev. Burns was a nephew of Robert Burns, Dunedin began with very distinguished, if tenuous, literary connexions. But this Burns, unlike his poet uncle, was a strict and austere Presbyterian,

and Cargill a forceful Scottish nationalist. The new colony in the south was to be founded on Protestant morals and dour Scots practicality. A visit to the Otago Settlers Museum, where the portraits of early settlers cover many walls, is a slightly chilling experience. No doubt early photography required that the subject sit very still, and precluded animation; but that cannot alone explain the grim rectitiude of so many of the faces.

Christchurch dates its beginning from the arrival of what the people of the region always refer to as the First Four Ships. The settlers landed at Lyttleton in 1850, and crossed the Port Hills to establish the new town on the Canterbury Plains. Again the settlement sprang from an idea of Edward Gibbon Wakefield's, though a separate company, the Canterbury Association, set up in 1848, had taken responsibility for it. Here the plan was that the settlement should be English, if possible exclusively Church of England, and that it should include immigrants of every stratum of society, something which Wakefield saw as both practical and necessary to the preservation of civilization in the colony.

The northern cities looked to have a better chance of success, in that there was a sizeable Maori population round about, and therefore a basis for trade – though what the long-term economic prospects were to be based on, apart from flax and timber, was unclear. James Stack, born in New Zealand in 1835, records that in the 1840s it was thought that the country might, like Argentina, develop an economy based on the export of tallow and hides to Europe (refrigerated meat being at that time undreamed of); and that consequently, like every son of a missionary, he was given, while still a small boy, a bull and a heifer as a beginning for what might become his herd.

In the 1860s the relative fortunes of north and south went briefly into reverse. While the northern settlements were threatened and hampered by increasingly militant Maori tribes, gold was discovered in Otago and on the West Coast. Between 1861 and 1863 the population of Otago increased from 12,000 to 60,000, and Dunedin became for a time the colony's largest town. Gold and wool established its prosperity, and when the wave subsided, and the pattern of settlement began again to favour the north, as it has continued to do, New Zealand was left with something that still looks like a small, perfect, Scots-Victorian city, kept lively and vital especially by its largely residential university.

Sudden developments, such as those the gold rushes brought about, were likely to conflict with the original plan of orderly settlement. Christchurch did not remain purely English and Anglican, nor Dunedin Presbyterian and Scots. Nevertheless, the visible signs of those origins are there. Christchurch has its willow-lined Avon river (and even – p170 – a student in a boater offering rides in a punt); it has Cathedral Square, Christ's College, and Hagley Park with its predominance of English trees. In 1940 Curnow wrote of the Avon:

> Which the English think looks English
> (Not reading between the willows)

– lines which are true and not true, and very much part of a literary push, characteristic of that time, towards the delineation of a distinct New Zealand character, which Christchurch's English pretensions compromised. Of course "reading between the willows" Christchurch is not English; it is a distinctly New Zealand city. But given its particular "look", what other parentage could we possibly ascribe to it? And if Alf's Imperial Army (p173) is a self-mocking parody of the Best (or the Worst) of British traditions, it is also a slyly ambiguous reassertion of them.

But the Christchurch suburbs are New World suburbs, running out in every direction from the centre of town, every family with its house and garden. There, as in all our cities and towns, the handicrafts which the pioneers practised still flourish – the ability to work the soil, to plant things and make them grow, to work with wood and glass and corrugated iron. "Do it yourself" may not be as near-universal as necessity once made it in New Zealand, but it is still widespread. And long views, especially on a good day the view from the Port Hills, across 60km of the Canterbury Plains to the Southern Alps, snow-white and crystal-clear in the distance, not only spell out very clearly to the eye and the understanding that this is not England; more importantly, they do something at once unsettling and challenging to the spirit.

So how did the Wakefield plans, so often derided, work out? Not of course as he hoped they would – but his hand is nevertheless visible in present-day New Zealand. The Taranaki settlement, despite the staunchness and courage of its English Westcountry settlers, was checked by Maori rebellion and guerrilla warfare; and though it recovered, it never caught up. Port Nicholson on the other hand did at last become the capital, as Wakefield had intended it should. Christchurch became a city, and Canterbury a region, which have never quite shaken off, nor been sure the wanted to, the "Englishness" he intended them to have. And Dunedin, which celebrates hogmanay and Burns Night with haggis and bagpipes, seems never to have objected to being Scottish in origin, so long as it was free to be Scottish in its own way.

The region which Wakefield had no influence upon, if only because it was never part of his plan, was Auckland; and Auckland has grown in size and wealth until economically, and even politically (since it returns so many Members to Parliament) it dominates the rest. That may be why Aucklanders are accused of believing that their green city in a benign climate between two harbours is the *real* New Zealand. It was the New Zealand no one planned, but which grew according to its own prompting.

Adventure, Space, Expectation

In a 1990 article discussing what has made the New Zealand character, Christine Cole Catley suggests three elements – adventure, space and expectation – and of these three the greatest (like Charity in the Biblical triumvirate) is adventure. The word seems right, if we add a few qualifications. Some adventures are chosen for their own sake, with no element of necessity. Someone may cross the polar ice, or climb Everest, or bungi-jump from the Eiffel Tower, "because it is there", or even from boredom. Every day young warriors with no more wars to fight take insane risks, which are a kind of adventure, on motorbikes or at the wheels of cars, and some are killed.

The adventure which set the earliest Polynesians sailing for these shores was not of that kind. It involved daring, skill and courage; but it must have included elements of necessity – either the absolute necessity of a storm and loss of bearings between islands; or the relative one of over-crowding on the home island causing war and want, and sending part of the population out in search of new lands. The same is true of most of our Pakeha forebears who set sail in the middle years of the nineteenth century, saying goodbye, most often for ever, to friends and family, packing up all they owned and travelling under appalling conditions for three months or more towards what was, from their point of viewing it, the world's remotest corner, a land occupied by a race known to be fierce fighters and only precariously brought to accept the settler presence and the British Crown.

The New Zealand Company, and others later, lauded the beauty of the place, its rich potential, its benign climate; but there must have been, in most of the settlers, some element of desperation which helped them to believe these promotional exaggerations. And when they reached their destination and for some "the pilgrim dream, pricked by a cold dawn, died", most of them set about bringing it to life again. The colonists, having invested in the project not simply what they owned, but their lives, their families and their futures, continued to live by the dream. These dreams, far more than European technology, were the secret power. By them they lived, and through them created the new nation.

When one contemplates the harshness of their lives – the mud, the forests, the absence of public facilities, the lack of every luxury and even of basic comforts, and above all the unremitting physical labour required by a very few people to make a huge territory over to an image of it they carried in their heads, one can see why the colonial mind so tirelessly insists upon its own good fortune. The dream must not be broken by the merest suggestion – especially one that comes from outside the fold – that it is not already the reality. Only by that insistence, combined with hard work, does it become in time, if not the reality, at least something close to it.

One emotion they must have had to cope with often was fear. Cannibalism is in itself, or in logic, no great matter; once I am dead it is hardly important whether my body is buried, burned or eaten. But it breaks a powerful European *tapu*, and the fact that the Maori traditionally engaged in human feasts after battle certainly figured in the minds of early settlers as something of a challenge to good relations and as a source of fear. My grandmother told me that her great uncle was taken by local tribespeople whom he had offended in some way. He was told that he was too thin to eat, but that he would be locked up and fed until he was fat enough – a piece of information that must have killed his appetite. After several days they said they despaired of his ever putting on weight, and let him go. It seems a good example of a kind of joke one recognizes as peculiarly Maori. Did he really believe he was going to be eaten? Possibly not; but there must have been moments, especially in the night, when fear got the upper hand.

Titokowaru, the Maori rebel whose guerrilla war very nearly brought about an end to the Taranaki settlement in the 1860s, understood this power of fear. It is thought that he did not practice cannibalism himself, though he apportioned the bodies of dead soldiers among his followers after a battle and let them decide whether or not these were to be eaten. But that is not the impression he gave the white settlers. Knowing the European horror of cannibalism (and indeed Maori themselves used it partly to humiliate an enemy tribe and to rub salt in the wounds of a defeat) he issued a statement, part of which read "Cease travelling on the roads . . . I have eaten the white man; he was cooked like a piece of beef in a pot. I have begun to eat human flesh, and my throat is continually open for the flesh of man. I shall not

die, I shall not die. When death itself shall be dead, I shall be alive."

To such challenges the Government forces had to respond, and were enticed to attack fortresses which proved to be so cunningly designed it was possible for a very few warriors to hold them successfully against a great number of assailants. And meanwhile Titokowaru's guerrilla bands ranged about the countryside, striking randomly, killing whole families in a single strike, stealing cattle and burning houses and barns. In the end the rebel chief was defeated not by the British soldiery (who assaulted his *pas* [fort] with great courage, and died in considerable numbers) but by his own *mana-tapu*. On the eve of an assault the Government forces were to make on Tauranga-ika, probably the best-designed and most impregnable Maori fortress ever built, the chief was found by his own warriors with another chief's wife. Confidence in his *mana-tapu*, and thus in their likely success in battle, was destroyed, and when the troops probed the Maori fortification in the morning it was found to be deserted.

This explanation for an otherwise inexplicable Pakeha victory is known to us only because of one of the most remarkable accidental adventurers in New Zealand history, Kimble Bent, whose story was first told by James Cowan. Bent, an American sailor whose mother was American Indian, had joined the British forces in Britain, been posted to India, and finally to New Zealand, where 50 lashes for disobedience completed a process that had taken him from disillusion, through depression to despair. He deserted to the Maori side, and for ten years he lived precariously as a Maori slave among the Hau Hau rebels. His reminiscences as told to Cowan have left us the only view of the 1860 wars through Pakeha eyes but from the Maori side.

Fear, then, and hard labour, were the negative side of the adventure of being a colonist. (Guilt only came later, and would have been incomprehensible to most nineteenth-century settlers.) Space, the second of Christine Cole Catley's three elements, was the source of a great deal of the sense of adventure. For more than a century every New Zealand child, even town children, grew up with it. Most town people had relatives they visited on farms. Picnics in various kinds of wilderness, swimming in the sea and in rivers, hill climbing, wandering (and getting lost) in the bush, fishing off wharves and bridges, off rocks and out of small boats, expeditions to gather *pipi* or mussels, eeling, blackberrying, mushrooming, rabbit-shooting, 'possum-trapping, – these, or some of them, used to be part of very nearly every New Zealand childhood. It is still almost impossible to find a New Zealander who can't swim; and many know what it is like to go close to drowning.

Most New Zealanders, during those first 100 years, came to consciousness in, and retained detailed and vivid memories of, a house surrounded by a garden, with other open land nearby and available winter and summer; so the first sense of self developed almost as much in relation to things as to people. To have some sense of control over a physical environment is a powerful builder of personal identity. It must explain, or help to explain, what lies behind that figure in literature (part mythological, but like all mythological figures, representative of a general truth), the silent New World man, socially neutral to the point, sometimes, of being a liability, yet whose presence in a room is strong and confident.

Unlike most places in the modern world, New Zealand includes extensive areas of wilderness it is still possible to get into and come to grips with. One does not look at "Nature" from a distance, or in a crowd, but experiences it in the most direct and physical way – swims in it, tramps over it, is scratched and bruised, doused and caressed by it. And it is this sense of immediacy of physical contact that expatriate New Zealanders miss more than anything else, and are unable to explain to anyone who does not share a comparable background. Where the typical New Zealander (whose forebears may have been Londoners) has differed most radically from the typical Londoner, is in being, comparatively, socially inept and physically competent. To exaggerate the case: I imagine the prototype New Zealander, lost in a big city, starving to death sooner than ask directions; while the Londoner, lost in the bush, would starve to death for lack of anyone to ask. Yet the faces of the physically competent are not often in themselves gifts to the photographer. To Werner Forman, New Zealand faces only usually in old age give the impression of having a story to tell.

Expectation was the third of Christine Cole Catley's key words – "the hope and determination that this would be a better society". The colonists who came here were not poverty-stricken and oppressed; but most were leaving behind a sense of constriction, of limit. They sought equality of opportunity, the chance to profit by their own labour; and all "radical" legislation in New Zealand has been to that end.

As the economic success of the colony waxed and waned, bringing troughs of the very kind of distress which emigration had been meant to leave behind, Governments enacted welfare legislation to ensure that citizens were protected. The most notable of these legislators, Ballance, Reeves and Seddon in the 1890s, Savage, Fraser and Nash in the 1930s, were not entirely lacking in a background of political and economic theory. Some, like Reeves, were widely read in it. But what characterized them was a pragmatism which drew upon theory not so much for its own sake as to justify what amounted to practical corrections.

The Liberals of the 1890s, nominally a party of individualism and *laissez-faire*, brought in legislation which helped to distribute land, to control working conditions and prevent exploitation, and to provide pensions for the poor and needy. They gave the state a role it had not previously had in the control of the economy and the amelioration of social distress, and in this they were credited with making New Zealand "the social laboratory of the world".

Labour, elected in 1935, was committed nominally to "the socialization of the means of production, distribution and exchange". It nationalized a few institutions; but its main achievement was the first comprehensive example of a modern Welfare State, and one which was protected as far as possible against the fluctuations of world markets by trade barriers and subsidies.

Since that time our most radically reforming legislation has been that of the Lange-Douglas Labour Government of 1984–89, nominally committed to the Labour tradition established in the 1930s, but in practice deregulating the economy, taking down protective barriers, removing subsidies, attempting to reduce the powers both of Government bureaucracy and of trade unions, and letting the winds of world trade blow through. Welfare protection would remain for the individual; but the economy was no longer to be protected by Government legislation and accumulating national debt. Once again the source was not political and economic theory; it was another case of pragmatism.

New Zealand has had, of course, long periods in which its legislators did nothing but oil the wheels, stoke the boiler, and check the guages. Conservatism has been the rule in our political life. But what has been notable when in two cases the shock of economic depression, and in the third the realization of perilously mounting national debt, has prompted politicians into radical action, has been the freedom with which they have been able to act. There is no established braking mechanism operating in New Zealand society. That same settler spirit which said if a forest got in your path you felled it or burned it off has been the source of our radical tradition, such as it is.

And the measure of our collective success has traditionally been a comparison with where we came from.

Colonial and Post-Colonial

After a visit to Australia and New Zealand in the early 1870s Anthony Trollope wrote that "as Auckland considers herself to be the cream of New Zealand, so does New Zealand consider herself to be the cream of the British Empire". He went on to say that this was a pretension to be found in every colony he had visited. "I remember that it was absolutely insisted upon in Barbados . . . that in Bermuda a confidence in potatoes, onions and oleanders had produced the same effect. In Canada the conviction is so rife that a visitor hardly dares to dispute it. In New South Wales it crops out even in those soft murmurings with which men there regret their mother country . . ." He goes on to say that this colonial confidence takes a special form in New Zealand, where the supremacy of England is acknowledged, and it is merely claimed that everything in New Zealand is like everything in England, but more so, and better. "I know nothing to allege against the assurance," Trollope writes. "It is a land happy in its climate; – very happy in its promises." But he adds, "I would observe to the New Zealander generally, as I have to other colonists, that if he would blow his own trumpet somewhat less loudly, the music would gain in its effect upon the world at large."

Can this colonial anxiety to assert superiority, to claim that we are especially favoured of the gods, and the accompanying clamour to have others from "overseas" confirm our good fortune – can these be entirely shrugged off as nineteenth-century phenomena, habits of our colonial past, now left behind? Here is a well-known New Zealand writer, in a text published 90 years after Trollope's:

> The human Kiwi, then. He has climbed Everest first. He has
>   often run the men of other nations into the ground
> on the Olympic track. He has built boats to jet up
> rivers where none have gone before. He has split the
> atom first, sent rockets to Venus.
> Of his ruggedness and bravery there is no question.
> He can be the only fighting soldier to win the Victoria
> Cross, for valour in action, twice in the twentieth
> century. That he has proved himself as a warrior his
> enemies would scarcely dispute.
> In the First World War New Zealand suffered more casualities,
>   in proportion to population, than any
> other nation involved. . .
> A man of action, then? Yes, but a dreamer too . . .

And so on. I don't quote this passage in order to deride it and seem superior. If these random assertions, at once shy and insistent, represent in crude and therefore usefully clear form some kind of national malaise, then it must be something which I share, or at least have experienced in my lifetime, and should be capable of understanding. That malaise is the condition of the colonial mind – the sometimes desperate-seeming search for praise and reassurance, commented upon by Trollope and many other visitors. It has its good and creative side. It is part of a process mentioned already – the bringing of something into being by unremitting insistence that it is so. But it is also, in its more extreme manifestations, a kind of neurosis.

Most writers these days will readily acknowledge the historical trauma of the Maori – a race whose culture has been supplanted, and even in some degree wiped out, by colonialism. What is not often considered is that, less obviously and less radically, but nonetheless significantly, the colonizers also suffer a trauma. The transplantation of European society into a new and alien environment produces deep anxieties which are not swiftly lost.

The first thing to be sorted out, and it happens only slowly, over many decades, is the relation to the Mother country. Because New Zealand's beginnings were gentler than Australia's, where the convicts and their descendants took one view of Mother England and the squatocracy another, and where the proportion of Irish Catholic immigration was much higher, New Zealand was for many years noted for its loyalty and patriotism. That is not to say, however, that everything went smoothly between London and the Government in New Zealand. There had always been differences between (to put it as it seemed from this end) settlers in New Zealand with their feet on the ground and policy-makers in London with their heads in the air – most notably in the matter of the signing of a treaty with the Maori in 1840. By the mid-1850s the colony was self-governing, but it was not yet independent; and it looked to England for imperial troops throughout the decade of the 1860s when Maori rebellion occurred – a war whose costs London did not enjoy meeting.

By about 1890 the number of New Zealand-born Pakehas exceeded those born outside the colony – a point in our development which the historian the late Sir Keith Sinclair considered of the greatest significance. From that time on, England as the source of so much of our cultural heritage became, for a majority of Pakehas, their Hawaiki – a place at once powerful, mythical and unreal, subject of famous novels and poems, where it snowed at Christmas and blossomed in May, and where the sun went around to the south; just as, in a different but comparable way, the English person who had never left Europe saw the distant colonies as mythical places, part of a great Empire stretching out into a hot incomprehensible darkness of tropical forests and cannibal feasts.

On both sides there were feelings of genuine goodwill, alternating, or existing side by side with feelings of resentment; and in some degree this has continued for more than 100 years. The New Zealander (like every colonial and post-colonial) has resented the sense of being claimed as some kind of imperial chattel, and yet at the same time undervalued, considered rough and untutored; the English have resented a corresponding representation of themselves as effete, impractical, over-refined, overbearing, snobbish. Caricatures have been perpetuated on either side; and yet each has made use of the other, when occasion demanded; and I think real bonds of affection and regard (not to mention family ties) have persisted, most notably in times of war.

By the middle years of this century, at a time when royal tours could still produce unparalleled enthusiasm and political assurances that "where Britain goes we go", there was already a well-established intellectual/literary tradition in New Zealand which scorned all such mindless enthusiasms and asserted a sturdy independence. The poetry of the 1930s and '40s, which established a distinct New Zealand literature, was founded partly on a profound, at times almost mystical, attachment to the local landscape, combined often with a satirical rejection of the oppressiveness of ties to Mother England. These two strands were present, for example, in A.R.D. Fairburn's long poem, *Dominion*, which seems at this distance sometimes crude in execution, but historically important in the way it catches the feeling of a land occupied a hundred years but seen almost for the first time, and of the necessary declaration of imaginative independence which was required before this clear vision became possible.

> In summer we rode in the clay country,
> the road before us trembling in the heat
> and on the warm wind the scent of tea-tree,
> grey and wind-bitten in winter, odorous under
> summer noon,
> with spurts of dust under the hooves
> and a crackle of gorse on the wayside farms.
> At dusk the sun fell down in violet hills
> and evening came and we turned our horses
> homeward through dewy air.
> . . .

> O Lovely time! when bliss was taken
> as the bird takes nectar from the flower.
> Happy the sunlit hour, the frost and the heat.
> Hearts poised at a star's height
> moved in a cloudless world
> like gulls afloat above islands.
>
> Smoke out of Europe, death blown
> on the wind, and a cloak of darkness for the spirit.

The colonial state of mind is always ambiguous. On the one hand it looks from a distance with longing or nostalgia towards the great centres where important things happen. On the other it sees those great centres (Europe in general, England in particular) as representing dirt, poverty, oppression and corruption – everything which emigration was designed to cure. Only the growth of confidence in a separate and viable national identity can gradually sort out this conflict of attitude and feeling. And our writers of the 1930s and '40s were merely one step ahead of the population at large in finding a New Zealand soul in the hills and on the plains where grass and shelter belts grew and the blackened stumps of former forests slowly faded into a transformed landscape.

Each decade seemed to bring a greater sense of independence. Our post-war defence ties, for good and ill, were more firmly with the United States than with Britain. But trade with Britain continued, and might have remained the country's chief foreign exchange earner if it had not been for Britain's entry into the European Community. Until that time we had thought it was for us to show signs of independence. Not to be wanted was somewhat chilling – but also salutary. New Zealand was forced to diversify its products and to go in search of new markets. The royal connection became more symbolic and constitutional than emotionally significant. The nation was now fairly on its own.

Independence – genuine independence – is good and welcome. We have all seen examples of the cultural cringe, and are glad if it is gone. A degree of deliberateness and self-assertion has been necessary. But there is a point beyond which nationalism cannot go without becoming foolish, destructive, and above all inauthentic. Things that happen of their own accord over time and by natural evolution tend to be more durable and less damaging than those which spring from intellect and theory, especially if underlying the theory there is an old, unresolved anxiety.

If after 150 years of European settlement New Zealand can be said to be in the grip of a new folly (and such is the norm of human societies) it is that of behaving as if time began in this place, and only 150 years ago; or as if geographical location determined cultural identity, and history and tradition were burdens to be shaken off. New Zealand is being reborn out of the liberal intellect, a "head-birth" (to borrow Günther Grass' phrase) the object of which is to invent for ourselves a new, non-British identity, Pacific and "bi-cultural". No one could object to that outcome if it should occur; but in the absence of any sign that time is bringing it about in the degree and with the speed thought desireable, it is being imposed from above, prescribed like a medicine and administered through education and the state bureaucracy, a prescription which, because it doesn't match most people's perception of reality, nor even very exactly their wish for what that reality should be, is bound, the more it is insisted upon, to be correspondingly resisted, and to exacerbate the very kinds of friction, especially racial friction, it is designed to cure.

What is most notable about this Government-sponsored programme is that all its elements, all its terminology, all its ideology, are imported from overseas. That which is supposed to signal our cultural independence signals that we are still cultural clients; while at the same time, in the interests of independence, we try to set aside as irrelevant to our present place and time those great works of English and European art, literature and music which are the best teachers of the only real freedoms – freedom of the intellect, of the imagination, of the spirit. Like most such follies, however, this one can probably be relied upon to pass.

To return, then, to those extravagant claims we have from time to time made for ourselves: It may be true that if one or several areas of human endeavour were considered – sport, for example, literature, soldiering, even scientific work – it might be possible to make out a case for New Zealanders, relative to population, having done better than many, or even most, national groups. I have no idea whether this is so; and if it is, it might be fair to point out that, given the large and productive area we occupy, and the relative peace and prosperity we have enjoyed, anything less would represent some kind of failure.

What does impress me when I consider New Zealand at large is the way a vast and wild landscape has been transformed into a productive garden, and how this was done mostly before heavy machinery was available, and by relatively few people. Modern New Zealanders are the inheritors of something achieved by the most prodigious efforts of physical labour. One might, with the judgment of our own time, deplore the bullying officiousness

it implies, the relative indifference both to the native ecology and to the indigenous people. But it would be ungrateful, and hypocritical, to complain of a history we all profit by. The making of modern New Zealand has been a momentous enterprise, well-intentioned, and bravely carried out. In that, and since the settlers were so predominantly British, our country might be seen as some sort of green monument to a great Empire, now gone. But why should the claim be made for one national, or even racial group? We are learning these days (aren't we?), however slowly and erratically, that we are human beings first, and only second Pom or Kiwi, Maori or Pakeha, Yugoslav or Dutch, Indian or Chinese. To look at it in that way, to see that huge garden as a reminder of what human beings have it in them to achieve, seems right and proper in 1990, and a way of lifting ourselves out of questions about identity which may have come to seem naive, or old hat. But the questions remain, and keep coming back at us in new forms.

By Sea and by Air

Always in these islands, meeting and parting
Shake us, making tremulous the salt-rimmed air;
Divided and perplexed the sea is waiting,
Birds and fishes visit us and disappear.
. . .
Remindingly beside the quays, the white
Ships lie smoking; and from their haunted bay
The godwits vanish towards another summer.
Everywhere in light and calm the murmuring
Shadow of departure . . .

CHARLES BRASCH

The British are islanders and have been traditionally seafarers and fishermen, a tradition which passed to the colony of New Zealand, except that sailing now became even more radically important than it had been in the homeland. Britain's nearest neighbour across the sea was so close a swimmer could reach it; New Zealand's nearest, Australia, was 2000 km away. The settlers had spent months at sea reaching New Zealand; and their way of life, and probably their lives, depended on the continual movement of ships to and from the northern hemisphere over those great expanses of water. As the colony established itself, economic viability depended on exporting by sea – and that, at least, has not changed.

Settlement to begin with was mainly around the coasts; and trade and travel were often more easily achieved by sea than overland. Harbours were crowded with small ships of every kind. Storms, shipwrecks and drownings were commonplace.

The total coastline of New Zealand has been estimated to be 10,000 km. No one lives very far from the sea. In the North Island the furthest point from the sea might be the centre of a huge lake, Taupo. Auckland is built on a narrow isthmus between two harbours. I remember in my childhood hearing a radio programme about surprising people and facts, which discovered a man who had crossed the North Island something like 30,000 times. He was a tram driver whose route took him back and forth perhaps eight times a day from the wharves at the bottom of Queen Street to the Onehunga Waterfront.

If you stand at the top of Mt Eden or One Tree Hill, there to the east lies the Waitemata Harbour and beyond it the islands of the Hauraki Gulf, and to the west the broad harbour enclosure of the Manukau. That view also gives you a feeling of why New Zealand has what I have always thought of, since I first went to sea, as "shipboard weather" – weather that seems to blow in from the ocean, blow across, and vanish away to the other side, followed by something different. You can stand in bright sunshine and watch westerly clouds close in over the Waitakere Ranges, completely shrouding them. The squall makes its way across the isthmus – Mt Albert, Sandringham, Balmoral, Mt Eden, the city and the eastern suburbs, and then away across the Gulf towards the Coromandel Peninsula – and we are in sunshine again.

Like the Maori, the settlers found themselves living in two elements, land and water, and to some extent it is still true. People rowed or paddled or sailed or (as time went on) used an outboard motor; in summer everyone swam. The tradition of sailing has remained strong, particularly in the north where Auckland likes to call itself the City of Sails, and where many millions of dollars are spent on yachts, and many millions in foreign exchange earned by yacht designers and yacht builders. New Zealand syndicates have challenged for the America's Cup, and won the One Ton Cup and other world championships; and at the moment of writing two Auckland ketches lead the fleet in the Whitbread Round-the-World Race, sailing 6000 km legs and arriving separated only by a matter of minutes.

Recreational and sporting sailing is the inheritance of a time when skill on the water was learned not by choice but of necessity.

Without exception it can be said that the experience of ocean sailing, even if only as passengers, lies somewhere in the family past of all of us. In my own case, one of my grandfathers was a Swedish sea captain; and among my mother's childhood memories was that of being allowed on deck in a storm, but tied by a length of rope to the mast, so that when a big wave came over she was (as she put it) "washed into the scuppers".

With that heroic age of sailing past, sea travel and wharves continued to figure in all our lives. Probably the most contentious industrial dispute in New Zealand history was that on the waterfront in 1951. If a waterfront union appeared to be gaining the upper hand, the country felt that that was a hand at its throat. Our economic life came and went through the wharves. But as important – perhaps more important emotionally – the wharves were our key to what would otherwise be (as it had been for the Maori) a locked door. You went to the wharves to farewell friends who were going abroad – "Home" as it was called if it was England (and it usually was) until that useage died out after a century of settlement. Streamers thrown from ship to shore, which stretched and broke as tugs pulled the liner slowly out into the stream and a band played "Now is the hour". You went to the wharves to welcome them home again, or to greet visitors and immigrants. These rituals were more poignant and terrible in time of war.

For those who travelled – and New Zealanders always did in large numbers – there was the strange business of packing, totally unlike packing for a modern flight. To go so far meant logically to go for a long time – it might even be for ever. You took almost everything you owned, the biggest objects nailed up in boxes marked "Hold", the medium stuff marked "Wanted on Voyage" and available in the baggage room, and the essential things marked "Cabin Baggage". Days and weeks passed at sea: storms in the southern oceans, boredom and heat and sleeping on deck in the calm of the middle latitudes, storms again in the north. You visited the Australian ports one by one; crossed the Indian Ocean to Ceylon or Bombay; travelled on to Aden; passed through the Suez Canal into the Mediterranean, where there might be stops at Naples and Marseilles; and then finally it was Tilbury Docks and London, where everything that had been encountered in books and had about it a consequent unreality, became visible and tangible at the same time that it retained, for a brief and magical few days, the feeling of being unreal.

Or the route, to or from, might take you through the Carribean and the Panama Canal. Even after the advent of modern fast ocean-going liners, the voyage was never less than four and a half weeks, and more often five. When my wife and I gave up ships and took to the air, we calculated we had spent a total of six months at sea. To have made by sea all the journeys I have now made by air would have taken me two and half years.

Now airports have become what the wharves once were. New Zealanders are still, perhaps more than ever, inveterate travellers. But when you can fly non-stop from Auckland to Los Angeles in 12 hours, and on to London in a further eleven, the world is no longer the place it was. We have removed ourselves from the sea into another element, through which we pass, uncomfortable, but largely desensitized. When we look down on Greenland and the northern ice, that is a magical experience, but one which teases the intellect while we take a drink and switch channels on our headphones.

I am grateful for the change. I am glad the world is more immediately available to us. But I know something has been lost – and it is not just the physical experience of the power of seas heaving a ship's bow up towards the heavens and then down into the trough; nor the beauty of the moon seen through rigging in the middle latitudes; nor the first sight from the sea of the immemorial and barren stones of North Africa; nor even the knowledge of just how vast the world is when it has to be passed over at 20 knots, day and night, mile by mile – though all those recognitions are indeed gone. More important, this ease and speed of travel, combined with the universality of international communication – direct dialling, satellite transmissions, instant news – has taken away from us the burden of isolation which was also an assurance of separateness and identity. It is as if in losing our old-fashioned and hated colonial status we have lost a treasure. The American poet Allen Tate once called internationalism the New Provincialism. To be at home everywhere it is necessary to be homeless. "In my end is my beginning." New Zealand's 1990 commemorations seldom felt joyful. It was as if we all felt weary with the knowledge that we had to begin all over again the painful effort of self-discovery.

It begins at sunrise

Our book opens at sunrise on the Treaty House (p 8). And here is Allen Curnow remembering a scene from his childhood, the sun rising over the Canterbury Plains:

Fluent in all the languages dead or living,
the sun comes up with a word of worlds all spinning

in a world of words, the way the mountain answers
to its name and that's the east and the sea *daas Meer,
la mer, il mare Pacifico,* and I am on my way to school

barefoot in frost beside the metalled road
which is beside the railway beside the water-race,
all spinning into the sun and all exorbitantly
expecting the one and identical, the concentric,
as the road, the rail, the water and the bare feet run

eccentric to each other.

We are all disposed to be pleased with Katherine Mansfield for having said "I want to make my undiscovered country leap in the eyes of the old world"; and for having written to her father from London, "I thank God I was born in New Zealand . . . New Zealand is in my very bones". But it doesn't do to forget the other Katherine Mansfield, witty and brutally honest, who recorded a wonderful dream of having booked her steamer passage home to New Zealand, which became a nightmare when she realized it was not a return ticket.

Good writers often have little reason to love their home country. Yeats records that for a couple of decades, living in London and published there, he never sent any of his books for review in Dublin, knowing they would be attacked, not on literary grounds, but because he was their author and his way of supporting the Irish nationalist movement was so complex and subtle it satisfied no one and angered many.

It is our writers, or rather a select band of those with exceptional talent, who have dealt best with the complexities of national identity, loyalty, and critical distance. In Maurice Duggan's story, "Along Rideout Road that Summer", the runaway teenager Buster O'Leary carries with him from his New Zealand Catholic schooling a British literary inheritance which remains in the forefront of his mind while he comes to terms with life on a Maori farm and with his first love affair. That inheritance becomes the intellectual and emotional frame by which everything gains richness and meaning. For him the landscape, the Maori girl playing her ukulele, the names of cows, even the label on the farmer's boots, all have literary echoes. There is an extra dimension to his world which protects him against the angers of his puritan parents when they arrive on the scene and try to persuade him to come home, but which also prevents him from merging into the simpler life lived by the Maori farmer and his daughter, which, at least in the language he knows, remains largely unverbalized.

Curnow's memory in the lines quoted above is of running to school "barefoot in frost beside the metalled road / which is beside the railway beside the water-race". To an outsider you would have to explain that the bare feet do not signal poverty (Curnow's father was an Anglican clergyman), but simply that the boy in question, running to school at about the time when Katherine Mansfield was making her undiscovered country leap in the eyes of the old world, was one of several generations of New Zealand children who, if they preferred to, went barefoot because it was something the informality of the Dominion permitted.

On the mind of the boy in the poem there are questions of languages and of naming, which seem to signal uncertainties of identity, place at odds with time and distance. The sun "comes up with a word of worlds all spinning / in a world of words" – and some of the languages are not English. Yet at least as strong as the intellectual perplexity (and enrichment) of his thoughts about language is the vividness of his sense of place, which is a language in itself, one that speaks direct to his senses as he runs to school. It is a scene which Curnow used in an earlier and simpler poem, where Time asserts:

> I am the nor'west air nosing among the pines
> I am the water-race and the rust on railway lines
> I am the mileage recorded on the yellow signs
>
> I am dust, I am distance, I am lupins along the beach
> I am the sums the sole-charge teachers teach
> I am cows called to milking and the magpies screech
>
> I am recurrent music the children hear
> I am level noises in the remembering ear
> I am the sawmill and the passionate second gear.

Most articulate and thoughtful New Zealanders, asked what for them represented their strongest and most enduring sense of "New Zealand", would, I'm sure, offer images like those which Curnow lays out and links up so casually and beautifully in those lines – physical experiences, sense memories, not cultural ones, nor social, nor political. They would be in almost every case positive. Yet there would be very little to say about them or make of them unless they were articulated by someone who could give them an intellectual and cultural framework.

Each area of the New World retains something of the period when it was first established. Australian intellectual and academic

life has always seemed to me to have about it something of a late Augustan flavour. Our own continues to be Romantic and Victorian. We are the inheritors of the English Romantic movement and of Victorian moralists. These have conditioned our education, our intellectual climate, our view of landscape, of the sea, of the Maori, of country versus town, and of moral and social responsibility. Probably every New Zealander at least has heard of the Treaty of Waitangi, while not one in 500 would have heard of Wordsworth's Preface to *The Lyrical Ballads*. Yet it would not be untenable, at least as a challenge, to argue that the latter more truly than the former is our "founding document".

A farmer's wife from Tauranga once told me that the world would not be much different if Shakespeare had never written. Of course it is true that life in New Zealand gets on very well, as it does in most places at most times, without consciousness of literary minds asking inconvenient questions about meaning and origin and identity. That life may be influenced in innumerable ways by intellectual forces; but it prefers to know nothing of them.

So let us return to Werner Forman's image of the sun coming up over the Bay of Islands and shining on the Treaty House, while clouds loom over threatening. What else is happening at this early hour? The Bay of Plenty farmer, whose wife frowned on the mention of Shakespeare, will have been up before the sun. The dogs have gone out and brought the cows in to the milking shed. Over the paddocks there is the chug and chuff of the milking machine and the sound of the bail opening to release the first cow, while the separator is already spinning to divide cream and skim. Before the first rays of sunlight have brought mist off the bush, sheep- and cattle-trucks are on the road to the meatworks. In town the auctioneers are at work in the fruit and vegetable markets, and fishing boats are heading out of harbour towards the open sea, where the latest container ship may be standing off waiting for the morning pilot. At Auckland airport traffic controllers are guiding in the first of several night-flights from Los Angeles.

There is a sense in which, for all New Zealand's present-day image of itself (stock-exchange, home and garden, fashion, cuisine, sophisticated drinking, fast travel) the day-to-day physical and emotional realities are only superficially changed: a great deal remains as it has been for the past 100 years. This collection of photographs offers a view of them as they appear through the eyes, and so through the camera lens, of one benign and talented European observer. We should all be interested to discover what he has to tell us about ourselves.

Looking towards Cape Maria van Diemen from Cape Reinga.

PRECEDING PAGE: Fishhook collected in 1793, probably in Doubtless Bay (known to the Maori as Tokerau), north of the Bay of Islands on the east coast, where the French explorer Surville came ashore in 1769. Doubtless Bay is still "undeveloped" (unexploited) – one of the most remote and beautiful places in the world, and still well-stocked with fish and shellfish.

This carved post (height 267 cm), named "Uenuku" and said to symbolize Uenukuwhatu, rainbow god of the Waikato people, is among the most interesting and prized of Maori *taonga* (treasures). So important is the object in Maori cultural life that the permission of Te Arikinui Dame Te Atairangikaahu, the Maori queen, had to be sought in order to reproduce it here. In its austere form, which seems to give it a special and mysterious power, it differs from most Maori carving, which tends to be intricate and rich in symbolic detail. It was found in 1906 in a swamp north of Te Awamutu (150 km south of Auckland, and 100 west of Rotorua). It has been claimed that it was carried to Kawhia harbour many centuries ago in the ancestral Tainui canoe, but the Forest Research Institute Laboratories have conducted tests which show it to be New Zealand wood – *totara*. It is possible, however, that it was copied from a more ancient version, since its design, though not unique, is untypical. There is an account of its provenance which says that it was hidden in the swamp during inter-tribal war, and that those who had put it there were not afterwards able to find it. It was discovered by a Pakeha (non-Maori) and, when put on display, was recognized and claimed by the family who were said to have hidden it. Posts of this kind, though rare, were sometimes used to mark important grave sites.

Silica sand dunes in the distance, seen from Parengarenga Harbour just below Cape Reinga on the east coast.

Whangaroa Harbour, Whangaroa Bay, just south of Doubtless Bay on the east coast, northern North Island. These remote northern areas are still largely occupied by Maori who retain their old tribal affiliations, meeting houses and *marae*.

RIGHT AND TOP RIGHT: A war canoe anchor stone (*punga* – length 40 cm) from Tatapouri, near Gisborne. Faces have been carved at either end of the dumbbell-shaped anchorstone. There are also designs to indicate ownership and that the stone belongs to a particular canoe.

Mt Taratara near Whangaroa Harbour, south of Doubtless Bay.

OPPOSITE: Giant *kauri* at Donnelly's Crossing. Waipoua Forest on the west coast just south of the Hokianga Harbour. This forest contains the best examples of thousand-year old trees, most of the rest in the northern North Island, where they flourished, having been milled out in the nineteenth and early twentieth century. The *kauri* (*Agathis australis*), a type of araucarian pine, grows to 30 m in height, old trees having an immense girth. It was used by the navy for spars, because it grew straight and tall; and was later valued as a building material. Its honey-coloured wood was also prized for furniture-making. In areas where the trees had been milled out *kauri* gum was dug from the soil, and used in making varnishes. In some parts of the Auckland region the *kauri* is regenerating well, now that milling is prohibited, though the opossum, introduced from Australia, may yet prove as dangerous to its survival as were the sawmillers of the last century.

Northern landscape inland from Spirits Bay
just south of Cape Reinga.

A wooden walkway allows visitors to go through this mangrove swamp along the estuary inland from the Treaty House at Waitangi. In the warm north the mangroves (*Avicennia marina resinifera*) grow 3 m in height. When the tide is out, the tubes (pneumatophores) through which the mangrove roots breathe can be seen – necessary because the mud in which they grow is largely anaerobic.

RIGHT: Stump of *kauri* kept at the Treaty House, Waitangi, probably taken from the swamp after many years weathering.

BELOW: Early morning, Haruru Falls on the Waitangi River. Not far below the falls the river spreads into a beautiful calm green tidal estuary which in turn, at its edges, becomes the mangrove swamp shown opposite.

The pattern in this piece of greenstone from the collection of items in the Treaty House looks like a night sky brightly lit by a moon partially obscured by clouds. By contrast the landscape is pitch black.

OPPOSITE: The Treaty House flagpole at Waitangi.

Evening light over Kawa Bay on the east coast near Warkworth, north of Auckland.

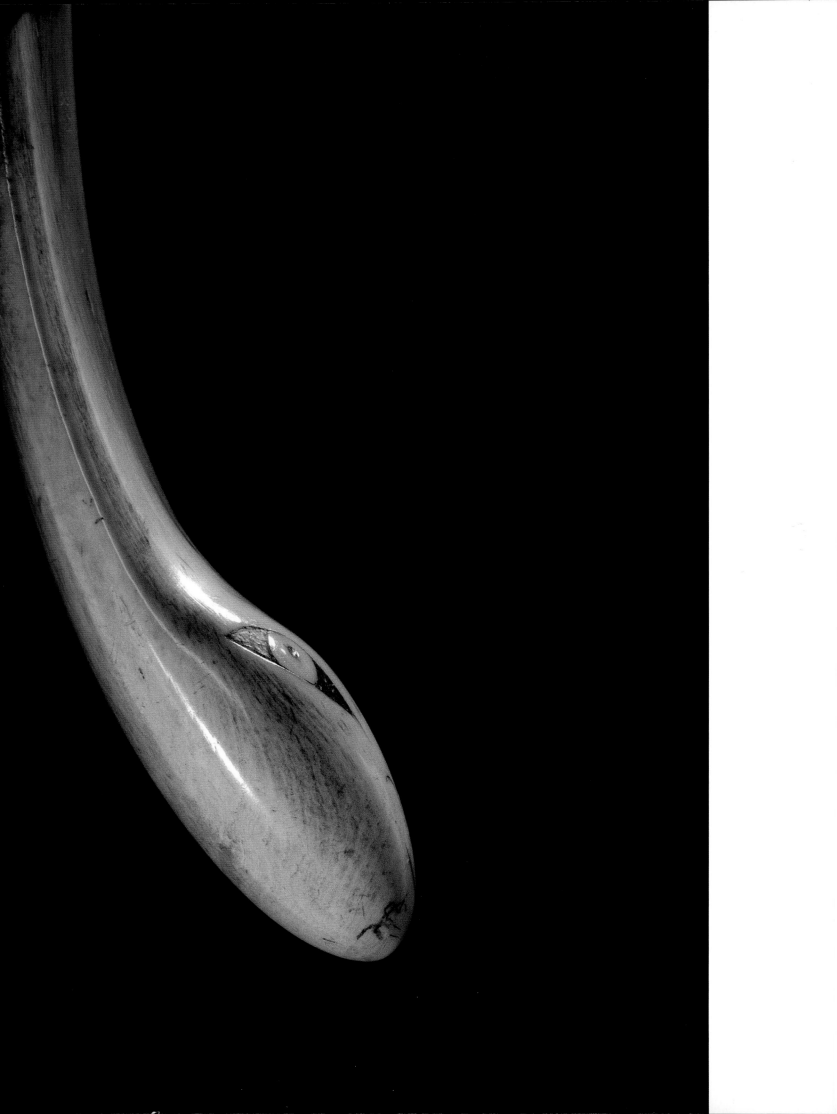

A carved wooden *patu*, or club, sometimes carried as a sign of *rangatira* (chiefly) status, and used for hand-to-hand combat in battle.

OPPOSITE: A whale ivory pendant worn by tribal chiefs. It represents a form of sea serpent and dates from the eighteenth century. Its characteristics link it with earlier examples discovered in Polynesia.

LEFT: A typical landscape of tree ferns (*ponga*) and *manuka* that spring up in the north when the *kauri* and other forest trees have been felled. The forest trees regenerate under that shelter of ferns and *manuka*. The location here is north of Auckland, near Warkworth.

BELOW: The spiral design carved into this oval treasure box (*wakahuia*) made on the east coast in the early eighteenth century, is said to derive from the tree fern, a piece of information which would puzzle anyone who had not cut one down. The design is not external to the tree, but is found, like tattoo markings, in the wood of the trunk when it is cut straight through.

OPPOSITE: Wiremu Wi Hongi, born 1909 and aged 80 when this photograph was taken. Mr Hongi is a *tohunga* of the Ngapuhi tribe. As a boy he was taught, and committed to memory, a great deal of the history and legend of his local sub-tribe. In 1935, possibly as a way of recovering from the serious dislocation that had occurred when he had been switched to a conventional European education, he wrote this knowledge out into notebooks amounting to about seventy pages. Recently these pages have been transcribed and translated into English by university anthropologists. Mr Hongi is tribal guardian of Lake Omapere, midway between Hokianga and the Bay of Islands.

56

ABOVE LEFT: *Putorino*, or flute-trumpet (eighteenth- or early nineteenth-century), played as a flute by blowing across the top, or as a trumpet by blowing into it. Either way it has one note which can be modified by closing the centre hole.

ABOVE RIGHT: *Putorino* made in two pieces lashed together.

OPPOSITE: Maori grave in Puketona Cemetery, east of Waimate, inland from the Bay of Islands. The "headstone", typical of Maori graves in the area dating from the early years of this century, is of carved wood in a style which seems halfway between Maori and European.

Evening, Hobson Bay, looking towards the city of
Auckland. Hobson Bay is one of the few of
Auckland's many inner-harbour tidal bays which
have not been "reclaimed" – filled and built over.
It is now protected and is a sanctuary for sea birds,
including oyster-catchers and grey herons, and also
the godwit, which feeds there briefly on its annual
trek from further south to Siberia via Japan.

The next four photographs are of "Alberton". It began as a relatively simple gabled farmhouse built in 1862 on the eastern slope of Mt Albert (Owairaka – one of Auckland's many volcanic hills) by Allan Kerr Taylor, who was born in Seringapatam, India, in 1832, the son of a General in H. M. Madras Army, and came to New Zealand in 1849. Alberton's ballroom, towers and balcony were added during the 1870s, designed by the architect Matthew Henderson, who drew inspiration from Kerr Taylor's Indian background. Kerr Taylor and his wife Sophia had ten children, eight of whom survived into adulthood. The property was originally 220 hectares. It is now kept as a museum, with appropriate "period" decoration and furnishings.

LEFT: "I passed this passageway, crudely sealed off with concrete, many times in the decades I visited Auckland University," writes Forman, "and its ugliness always irritated me. What a pleasant surprise to find that some students felt the same way and did something about it!"

BELOW: Eighteenth-century *toko wananga* (symbols of gods), which were placed outside a house of learning to indicate what was being taught, and to attract the appropriate god who would settle on the head of the stick. The twisted stick represents Tawhirimatea, god of storm winds; the straight stick is Tumatauenga, god of man and war; the stick with one swelling is Tane, god of the forests; and the wavy stick is Tangaroa, god of the sea. This set, found in the Waikato region, South Auckland, is unique.

OPPOSITE: University of Auckland – the clock tower on the old Arts Building, known locally as "the wedding cake". The building was designed by R. A. Lippincott and built in 1929 for £150,000. Despite its pseudo-Gothic appearance, there are local details. The arches over the entrances are decorated with representations of flax seed pods; the crockets are the shapes of *ponga* fronds; the bosses are New Zealand birds – kaka and kea. (See also p 14 for further discussion of this photograph.)

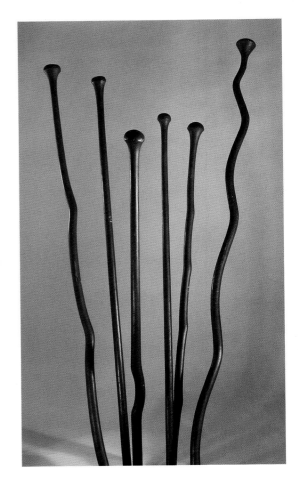

Last interment in the churchyard of the tiny St Stephen's chapel that looks over Judges Bay, Auckland. It was built in wood in 1847 to replace an earlier stone chapel which collapsed because sea sand was used for cement. Mrs Sarah Selwyn, wife of the Bishop and church builder, records that the chapel (which must be one of the smallest ever built) had been put there "chiefly for the Maoris who used to bring their canoes in the early days into the little bay and camp out on the shore. There was a little Maori Hospital on the shore provided for and attended by the kind Martins" – (Martin being the name of New Zealand's first Chief Justice, who lived there and caused the bay to be named as it is).

OPPOSITE: The grave text, so strangely (and typically) alight in Forman's photograph, seems illustrated by his next, showing the masts of the barque *Tui*, originally a coastal trader, then a sugar lighter operating out of Auckland after the First World War. It is now permanently moored on the Waitangi estuary, not far from the Treaty House, and open to the public as a Museum of Shipwrecks.

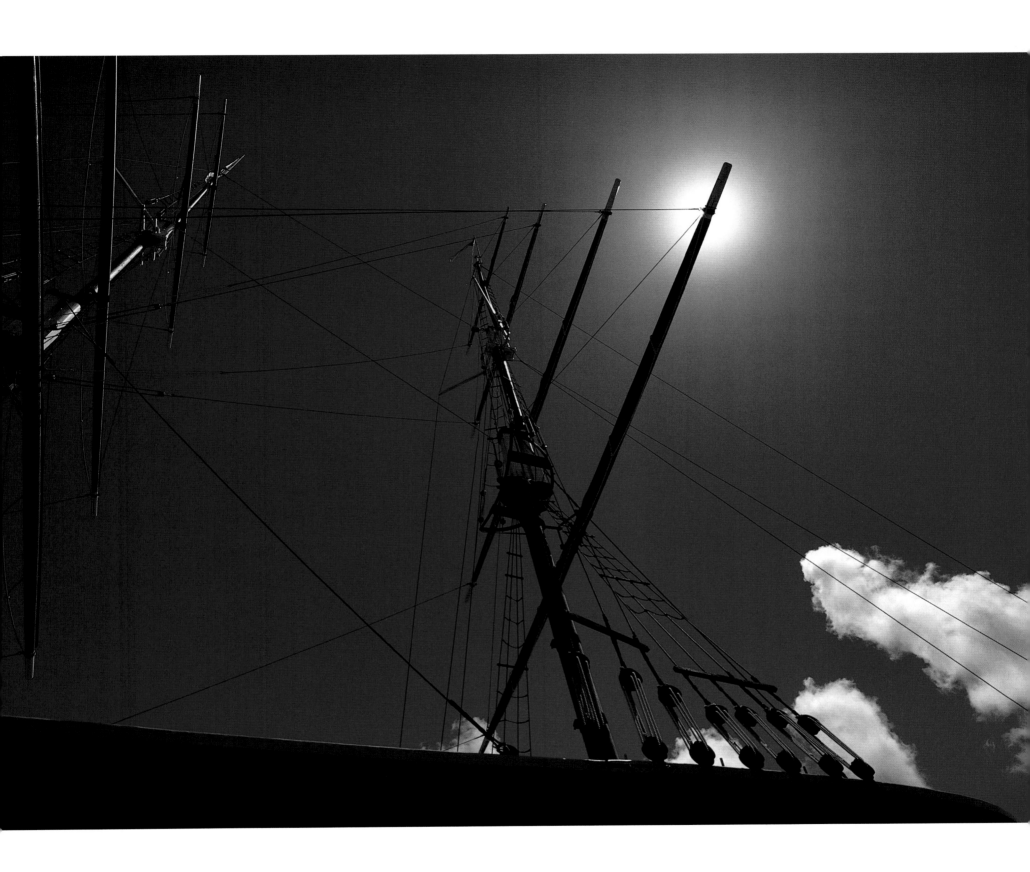

Painted war-canoe paddle, collected by
Captain Cook on the east coast of the North
Island in 1769. Unlike Polynesian paddles,
Maori paddles have a long, flat blade. The
wood's natural surface has been used to
make the pattern, while the background has
been coloured with red ochre mixed with
shark oil.

LEFT: Whitbread Round-the-World yachts
leaving Auckland, 1990, on the leg that
would take them round Cape Horn. Across
the Hauraki Gulf can be seen the island
of Rangitoto.

Sheena, five and a half, born in Auckland of Niuean parents. Forman writes: "This image of radiant *joi* recorded at Waitemata coincides with Niue's great devastation [by storm] on the same day".

OPPOSITE: Sir Edmund Hillary (b 1919) the former beekeeper who in 1953, on the eve of the Queen's coronation, became famous as the first man to set foot on the summit of Everest. Later he joined Sir Vivian Fuchs to make "the last great journey in the world", a crossing of the Antarctic continent through the South Pole, the journey which had defeated Ernest Shackleton. Sir Edmund has spent a good deal of his life, since his early adventures, working to raise money for, and help build, schools and hospitals for the Sherpa people of Nepal. He served a term recently as New Zealand ambassador in India. He is much loved in his home country, and is the only living New Zealander to figure on the new bank notes. In this photograph Forman catches what he calls "the tougher than an old boot image".

Nikki Jenkins, 14, Commonwealth Games Gold Medallist, 1990 – the first New Zealander to win an international gold medal in gymnastics.

OPPOSITE: Dame Louise Henderson, distinguished New Zealand painter, born in Paris 1902, came to New Zealand as a young woman to marry a New Zealander. She returned briefly to Paris in 1952 to study under the Cubist, Jean Metzinger, and made a significant contribution to the modernization of the New Zealand art scene during the 1950s and '60s.

Evening – Auckland skyline from Parnell.

The Auckland Harbour Bridge seen at night from Herne Bay. Built as a four-lane bridge in 1959, it opened Auckland's north shore, previously accessible only by ferry, or by road 50 km around the harbour, to suburban development, and soon had to be enlarged to take eight lanes, now once again considered insufficient.

OPPOSITE: Recent building in Wellesley Street, central Auckland, including Orient Towers on the corner of Kitchener Street, built in traditional style by a New Zealand-Chinese business family.

The top floors of the Fay-Richwhite Building (late 1980s) on Queen Street, central Auckland, seen here through the branches of a pepper tree from the high ground of Albert Park. To many, some approving, others not, the still relatively young merchant banker, Sir Michael Fay, of Fay-Richwhite, symbolizes "Auckland" – money, sailing and the good life. He is the first New Zealander to have challenged for the America's Cup.

OPPOSITE: Evening – Auckland city skyline across Hobson Bay.

Korowai or feather cloak worn over the shoulder by *rangatira* (chiefly persons) on ceremonial occasions. The Maori had many different kinds and styles of cloak, each differently named. "Korowai" indicates that this one, made by finger weaving, has black thrums. The feathers are from various birds – kaka, kiwi, and others. Forman notes that the black fibres and bright feathers "create, with their own shadows, a kinetic and near-psychedelic effect".

OPPOSITE: This primitive pedestrian tunnel under the old railway track through lower Parnell leads to a path through woods, known locally as the Ho Chi Minh Trail, on the lower slopes of the Auckland Domain. Forman's note reads: "Flare-up on the Ho Chi Minh Trail. Locked in combat are the forces of Deanna, nine, and Philip, ten."

Sisters, fifth generation New Zealanders: Young Auckland lawyer, Charlotte (OPPOSITE), and law-student, Margaret (ABOVE). Their earliest New Zealand forebear arrived in the Bay of Islands in 1834, and their antecedents are English, Scottish, Welsh, Catholic Irish, Protestant Irish, French and Swedish.

LEFT: Lize Jaeger, 93, came to Kaihere from Latvia in 1925 bringing spinning wheels that had been used by her grandmother and mother. She is seen here with her great granddaughter Jessica, three and a half, whom she hopes soon to teach to use the wheel.

OPPOSITE: A back garden, Bradford Street, Parnell, near central Auckland. Forman celebrates the old materials of the first hundred and more years of Pakeha architecture – wood, weatherboard walls, and corrugated iron roofing. The garden of mixed English (deciduous) and Pacific (evergreen) trees and plants is enclosed by a now rusting and dilapidated corrugated iron fence.

BELOW: These materials were used not only for rudimentary architecture, but for elaborate homes as well, as this detail of weatherboards and wooden balusters with hollyhocks and roses at Alberton shows.

Prudential looks down its nose at Orient Towers, which Forman calls "a pagoda consecrated to the deity of profit"; but news reports shortly after its completion suggested that the deity had yet to deliver.

OPPOSITE AND OVERLEAF: Two Auckland examples of cinema interiors from the great age of picture palaces – the St James Theatre, and the Civic. The Civic in particular, built 1930, has an extravagant grandeur of design equal to some of the famous cinemas in Hollywood. Its interior represents a Moorish city with walls, towers and minarets, and a dark blue night sky overhead in which the stars shine and wink. The eyes of the lions on either side of the screen glow red and fade. Before a recent reconditioning the wurlitzer organ used to spiral up into view out of a well, and a "gondola" in the Wintergarten Cabaret below the picture theatre came up out of a pit bearing a full orchestra.

FOLLOWING PAGE: Looking up from the roof garden of the Chase Plaza, central Auckland, towards the Simpson Grierson Building (both late 1980s).

Detail of a red carriage.

LEFT: Railway tunnel through Parnell. Forman comments:
"Red carriages of the once-in-a-blue-moon train can be seen
exiting from the far end."

Te Porere Redoubt, south of Lake Taupo and just west of Lake Rotoaira, built by the (in the eyes of Pakeha and Kupapa) murderous rebel, or (as his followers saw him) visionary leader, Te Kooti Rikirangi Te Turiki, for what was in effect his last full-scale battle with his Government and Kupapa ("friendly Maori") pursuers in October 1869, at the end of what had been a long year of guerrilla warfare. After that battle Te Kooti was pursued further but vanished into the heartland for more than a decade, after which he was pardoned. Although Maori methods of fortification are said to have been copied by European military strategists, and although Te Kooti was one of the most effective of Maori guerrilla fighters against the Crown, he is not credited with much success in the design of defences, and this one was fairly easily breached. (Part of Forman's interest in this particular photograph is in the variations of green under what he describes as "streaky light".)

Matua Tonga on Mokoia Island, in Lake Rotorua. This Kumara god of fertility is said to have been brought from the legendary homeland, Hawaiki, in the ancestral Arawa canoe.

RIGHT: *Waka* (canoe) built by Rotorua carvers. Mokoia Island is in the background.

Ohinemutu is the only Maori village existing as such on its original site within a modern town (Rotorua). "Kuini Wikitoria" presented the statue of herself to the Arawa tribe in recognition of their loyal support of the Crown during the wars of the 1860s. Carved in stone, it has been honoured with an appropriately Maori surround of painted and carved wood, and set by a hot lake-edge which from time to time envelops it in sulphurous fumes.

The boy is the grandson of Mrs Moore, who appears opposite, and Mrs Moore is the oldest surviving grand-child of the rebel chief, Te Kooti. Mrs Moore is present custodian of Te Kooti's *mere*, and other Naora family *taonga* (valued treasures), a custodianship which, it is expected, will pass to her grandson.

Here Forman's passions for aircraft and photography combine. He flies over Inferno Crater (87°C), Waimanga Thermal Valley, in the central North Island, on a cool calm morning and records that the 50-year-old Tiger Moth, long ago taken out of service and only recently restored, is gently buffeted by rising hot air – "a signal in the lake's morse code, saying Happy Birthday to a moth who got her wings in March of '39."

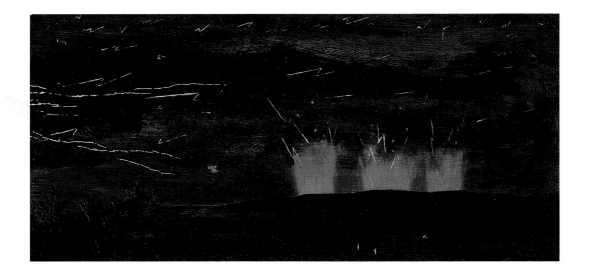

TOP: Julia Maude Bennett's instant record of the Tarawera eruption of 1886 as seen from Te Puke. She was not a painter, but grabbed a piece of cardboard and recorded what was happening 50 km away. (See p 23 on the subject of this eruption.)

ABOVE: Te Horou ("the Cauldron") of Whakarewarewa, Rotorua. The temperature of this spring is over 80°C and its level is constantly changing.

RIGHT: The crater of Mt Tarawera seen from the air, showing the split in the mountain caused by the eruption of 1886.

Tikitere (also known as "Hell's Gate"), Rotorua region. Steam can be seen rising from the lake which in places reaches temperatures of 115°C.

The house of the *tohunga* Tuhoto Ariki at Te Wairoa, the village buried by the Tarawera eruption; and stone storehouse for food (see pp 22–23 for the story of Ariki's fate).

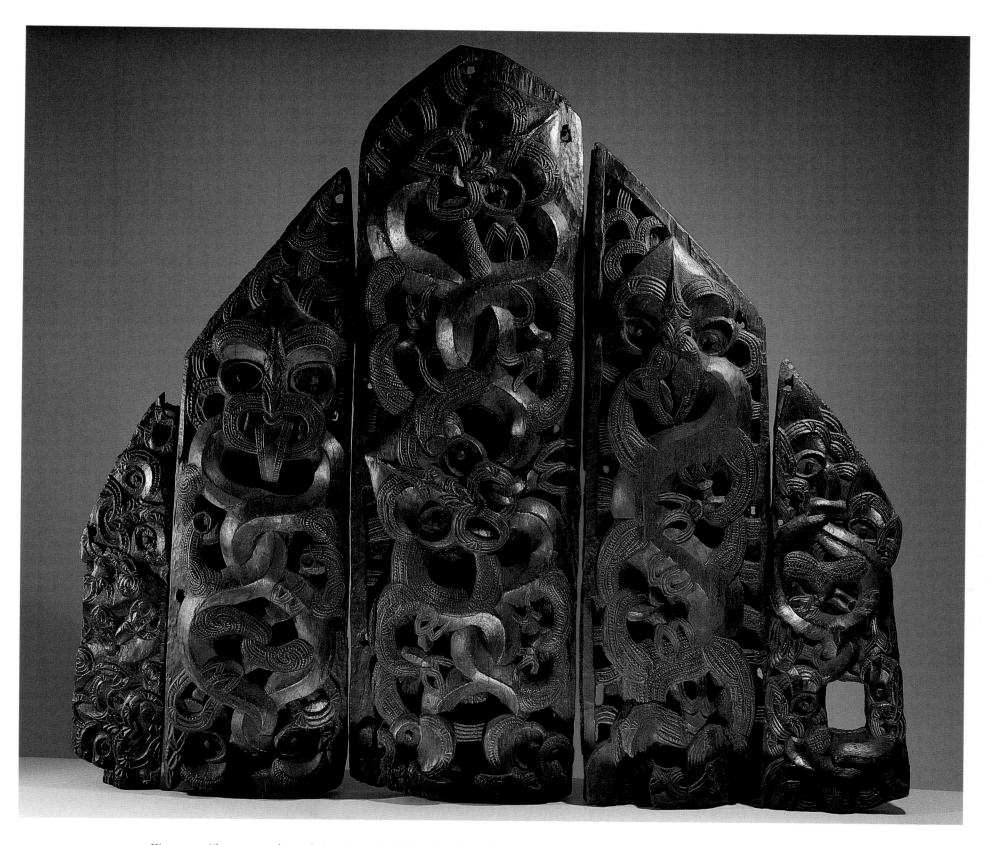

Five magnificent carved panels (1.26 x 1.48 m) from the front of a *pataka* (storehouse). Made in the classic Taraniki style, they are the only full house-front of this period and quality to have survived. In the monumental central panel one *tiki* figure stands upon another, their heads typically side-tilted, their limbs, three-fingered hands and feet interlocked. The two larger side panels present a pair of male and female *tiki*. At the base are the *manaia* figures; half avian, half human, they suggest a subtle and involved relationship with ancestral gods. A whole universe of *mana* (spiritual essence) is contained in these five panels. To the Maori, the *mana* of any object, animate or inanimate, was of paramount importance, to be closely guarded by elaborate and careful rituals, and surrounded with *tapu*. Food stuffs in particular and priceless things could be housed only in a building of the most sumptuous design; the *pataka* performed for the community what the treasure-box did for the individual. Many of the surviving fragments have been found in swamps near Waitara, presumably hidden from tribal enemies or European settlers.

Life mask taken in 1854 for Sir George Grey of Chief Tapua Te Whanoa of the Ngati Whakaue *hapu* (sub-tribe) of the Arawa *iwi* (larger tribal grouping) of the Rotorua region, showing full facial *moko* (tattoo) done with little adzes of bone dipped in liquid charcoal and struck with a tapper.

LEFT: Ferns and forest trees on the river bank near Te Wairoa, the buried village.

PRECEDING PAGE: Sunlight and cloud shadow, seen from the Kaimai Range coming down towards the Bay of Plenty and Tauranga.

OVERLEAF: Ngongataha Valley, west of Rotorua. (The New Zealand Wool Board sells about one million kg of wool for every day of the year, and the sheep population varies between 70 and 100 million. "That is," comments Forman, "given a total population of three and a half million, about 25 sheep for every New Zealander.")

Kaingaroa Caves, discovered in 1925 in the course of burning off preparatory to planting what has become the Kaingaroa Forest. Forman's note on this photograph is as follows: "The Ngati Manawa who inhabited this area for some 400 years had no knowledge of the existence of these caves, and it is thought the carvings may be some 700 years old, depicting the traditional 'Great Fleet' migration to New Zealand. The zig-zag lines on this cave wall are the same as the ancient Egyptian hieroglyph meaning sea or water, used both in paintings and reliefs depicting the sea or waterline. In writing it spells 'n' or 'nun', meaning water. This is the more astonishing since both traditions were perfectly able to carve the more realistic wavy line, as can be seen on this relief carving, yet both, for whatever reason, used a zig-zag line to represent water."

BELOW: The cave shelters a Maori canoe, an undistinguished river craft.

LEFT: Canoes at sea carved in the Rhyolitic bluff of the cave shelter.

This model war canoe was made by a Gisborne carver in the mid-nineteenth century.

The central fragment of a lintel of a chief's house, which was carved in the East Cape region in about 1800. It shows a human figure in the middle, with two *manaia* at the sides. It is decorated with *taratara a kae* notches.

RIGHT: Beach below Mt Maunganui at the entrance to the Tauranga Harbour.

OVERLEAF: Foothills of the Kaimai and Mamaku Range between Rotorua thermal region and Bay of Plenty, illustrating the importance of shadow as well as light in Forman's photographs.

Probably carved in the early part of the nineteenth century, this lintel belonged to a house that stood on a small island *pa* (fortified settlement) at the western edge of the swamp which, now drained, is the Hauraki plain. It is unusually large for a stone-tool carving. The central figure may represent Hine-nui-te-po, the death goddess, just before Maui tried unsuccessfully to attain immortality by (as Forman puts it) "reversing the process of birth" – re-entering the womb while she slept. She was woken by the laughter of fantails and closed her legs, killing him. (See also text p 15.)

OPPOSITE: This monument-sized *tiki* surmounting the gateway to Ohinemutu, on the south shore of Lake Rotorua, represents Pukaki, one of the principal Te Arawa ancestors, and his two sons. The carving is in the traditional Arawa style with a realistic facial tattoo.

An early canoe prow from Doubtless Bay in the far north. The sculpture is transitional between archaic and later Maori art.

LEFT: Looking towards Napier from Cape Kidnappers, so named by Captain Cook because local Maori tried to kidnap a young Tahitian boy sailing on the *Endeavour*.

The mountain range which Maori legend says is a
sleeping chief – Te Mata peak in the foreground, the
Tukituki River and Hawke Bay in the distance.

Rotoehu forest in the Rotorua region – thermal emissions mixing with smoke from a forest fire to produce mushroom clouds.

OPPOSITE: Evening light, Wairoa Valley between Lakes Tarawera and Rotorua.

The interior of Te Hau-ki-Turanga meeting house built at Manutuke near Gisborne in 1842, and now displayed in the Museum of New Zealand in Wellington. The house represents an ancestor whose backbone is the painted ridge pole, partly supported by the free-standing figure (see detail) representing another ancestor.

OPPOSITE: The front of the storehouse of Te Puawai o Te Arawa which was carved by Wero Taroi of the Te Arawa (a well-known carving *hapu*) and built for Te Pokiha Taranui in 1868. It stood at Maketu in the Bay of Plenty and is now displayed in the gallery of Auckland Museum. It is said to be the last great Maori storehouse to be built in the old style. The central figure represents Tamatekapua, chief and founder of the Arawa tribe from Hawaiki.

After the earthquake of 1931 Napier Theatre, known as "New Zealand's finest Opera House", was a ruin in the centre of a virtually wiped-out city. To rebuild the theatre a competition was organized and the best design, the project submitted by J. A. Louis Hay, was chosen. Hay had won the competition – but lost the job. The cost of £15,000 for a house to seat 1150 (i.e. a cost of £13 per seat) seemed extravagant. The borough architect was awarded the contract to build it on the cheap. Still, today Napier's is the one outstanding Art Deco Theatre left in New Zealand. Forman comments: "The price of a seat has grown exponentially and now costs twice the original per-seat construction price of £13 merely to hire for an evening."

OPPOSITE: Art Deco style administration of the National Tobacco Company built in 1935 in the reconstruction following the Napier earthquake of 1931. Now Rothman's New Zealand headquarters. Forman remarks: "A design and execution careful in line and detail but overall clean and simple results in an approach, an individual means of access, a perfect doorway. The more surprising since it is a part of a warehouse complex within the square mile of warehouses of Napier's harbour. Where else can one find a comparable dockland edifice?"

Wooden chimney of a shed used to smoke meat, fish and cheese. Forman comments: "Dissatisfied with man's strict utilitarianism, nature adds a touch of its own Art Deco."

Butcher shop, Ongaonga, south of Hastings, an area settled by Scandinavians. Forman says: "A far cry from modern shopping mall eyesores. Charm and style in the midst of a godforsaken rural nowhere."

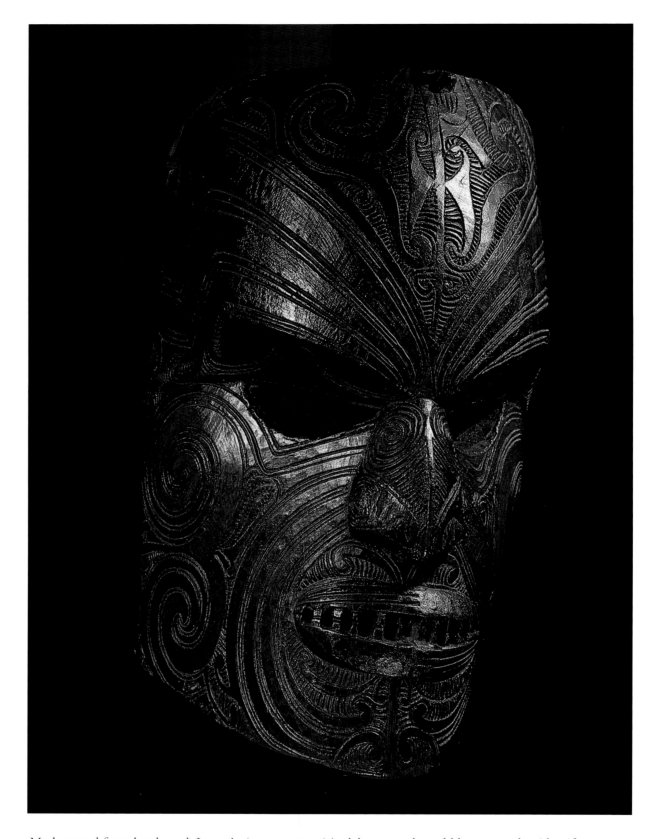

Mask carved from hardwood. Its *moko* (tattoo pattern) is elaborate and would have served to identify a person of rank. Forman comments: "Masks were made and used all over the Pacific, but surprisingly Maori art appears to have produced only this fine example."

OPPOSITE: Duane Nathan. Forman found him in a pub, whose clientele appeared to be exclusively Maori, near the Te Aute College, famous as the educational establishment which produced many of Maoridom's great leaders. An old Pakeha woman who lived next to the pub told Forman that Maori youth in the area feel "spiritually kindred to the Ringatu of the Upraised Hand", and so to the nineteenth-century renegade chief, Te Kooti.

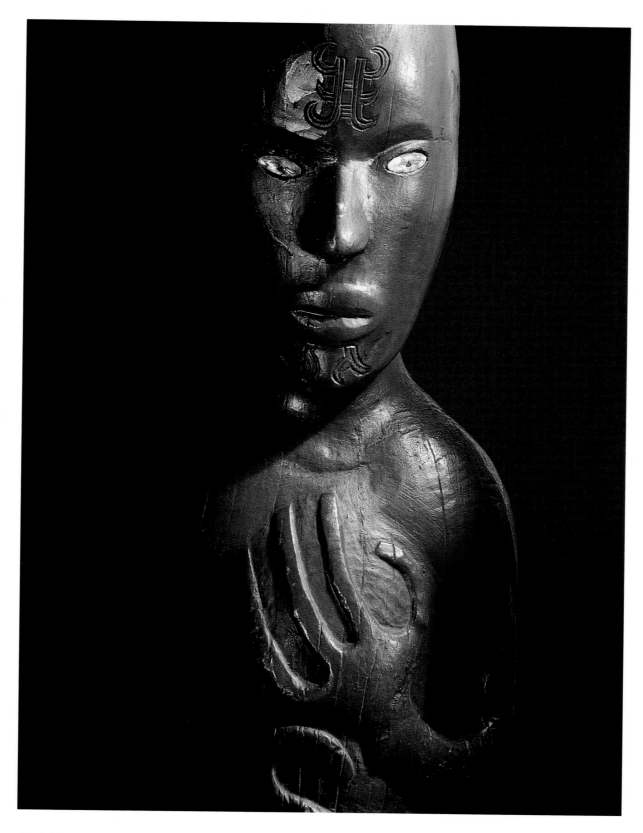

Probably carved about 1860, this ancestress is a ridge-pole support (*poutokomanawa*) of an east coast style house, though the tattooing on the chin is in the west coast style fashionable at the time.

OPPOSITE: It is possible, however, that there would not be a lot in common between the Maori schoolboys of Te Aute College, and the young Maori men in the local pub. Apirana Taylor has a poem about a Maori youth who knows almost nothing of his own language and culture and must speak on the *marae* (tribal forum), which includes the following lines (Ngati is tribe; DB is a brand of beer; *taiaha* is a spear):

Then I spoke
My name is Tu the freezing worker
Ngati DB is my tribe

The pub is my *marae*
My fist is my *taiaha*
Jail is my home

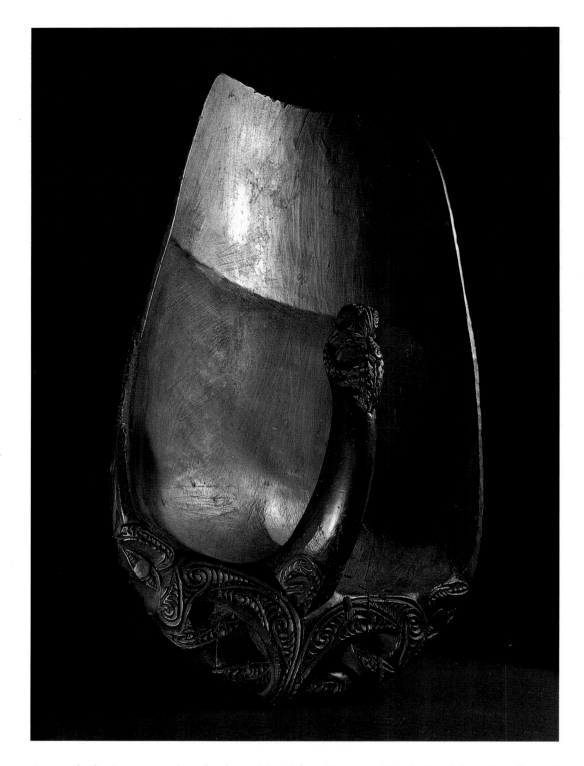

A canoe bailer (47.5 x 30 cm) made of gourd (*taha*) from Tomoana, Hawke Bay. The priapic form of the handle is surely not accidental. War canoes up to 25 m in length were made with a dug-out hull and end-pieces, topped with side-strakes. Holes were caulked and there were covering battens, but leaks were unavoidable. Men with bailers sent out cascades of water from the wells made in the platform for the paddlers' feet. The canoe would not sink if swamped but would wallow.

PRECEDING PAGES: Carved wooden bone box (*atamiro*) for the burial of human remains (125 x 33 x 22 cm) found in the Raglan area on the west coast of the North Island. Such boxes are considered extremely *tapu* (sacred) objects which should not be on general display, and which some Maori believe should be returned to the place of their former burial or concealment.

OPPOSITE: Maori carver, Vince Rerard, of Waipa Kokiri Centre, Te Awamutu. Traditional Maori wood carving (using modern tools) has been revived in recent years, partly as a way of keeping Maori culture alive, and as a manifestation of pride in Maori culture.

The *taumata atua* (shrine) of the god of agriculture, Rongo. The sculpture was a visible symbol to the god that his aid had been invoked to ensure a good crop of *kumara* (sweet potatoes). It came originally from Waitara in North Taranaki.

RIGHT: The Mokau River near Piopio. It links the interior of the King Country with the Tasman Sea.

PRECEDING PAGE: This photograph of Taranaki in early morning light very nearly cost our photographer his life. See pp 14–15 of the Introduction for details.

Characteristic earlier style (probably late nineteenth-century) Wellington house, built in wood among the slopes and gullies which are always too steep to be completely gardened, and consequently give even areas close to the central city a less-than-completely urban look.

PRECEDING PAGE: Of all the New Zealand towns and cities Wellington, with hills rising steeply all around, offers the most spectacular harbour views; and the hills, pressing in above Lambton Quay, give its relatively modest business district a touch of big-city compression.

OPPOSITE: Twentieth-century Wellington rising behind, and looming over, nineteenth-century Wellington.

Modern domestic architecture in Wellington.

RIGHT: This is mundane Wellington down on the flats, seen from Mt Victoria, with characteristic wooden houses and painted iron roofs in the foreground.

Typical old-style Maori pallisade fence of *manuka* stakes at the Tapu te Ranga *Marae*, Island Bay, Wellington. Clearly this place and what went on there took Forman's fancy more completely than anything else he found at the southern end of the North Island – which, it should be remembered, since it goes visually unrecorded here, is also our seat of Government. The remaining photographs in this section (with the exception of the bone *pekapeka* on p 152) were all taken at the *marae*.

OPPOSITE: Bruce Stewart, Maori writer, born Hamilton 1936, who says he graduated from prison in 1972 to found the Tapu te Ranga Marae. As a writer, Stewart is chiefly known for a prison story "Broken Arse", which he also made into a play.

Not a traditional tattoo, either, on Richard Ngatai's arm, but typical of those worn by Maori gang members, usually acquired during prison terms, and worn as badges of distinction. One of Richard's reads in pseudo Sanskrit, "Dream Evil". He was born in Gisborne in 1969 and is a builder.

RIGHT: Human bone *pekapeka,* two-headed and armed breast ornament, c. 1850, from the Wellington area.

Construction of the new meeting house nearing completion. Forman observes that the *marae*, "put together from waste, also recycles human material that society has cast aside".

Communal building – clearly not quite a traditional *whare*; but this and other buildings and fences are largely constructed of wood from US and Japanese car containers and similar material recovered from waste tips.

OPPOSITE: The *marae*'s support pole. Forman's note reads "for communications by wire and spray can".

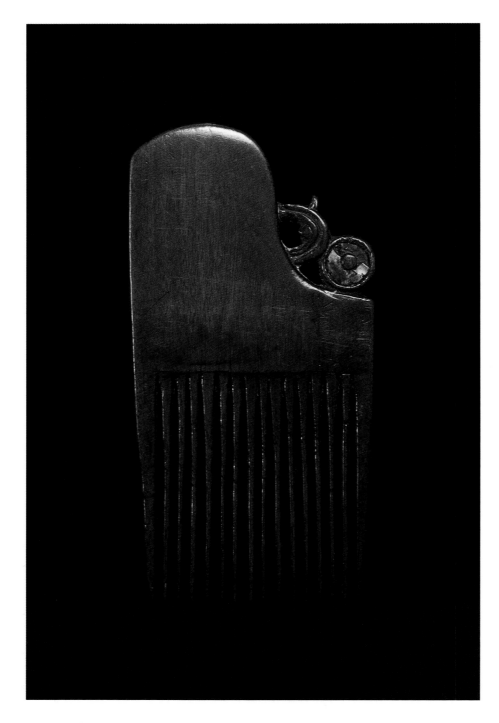

An unusually small and finely-carved eighteenth-century wooden hair comb of a kind worn in a man's topknot and often painted with red ochre.

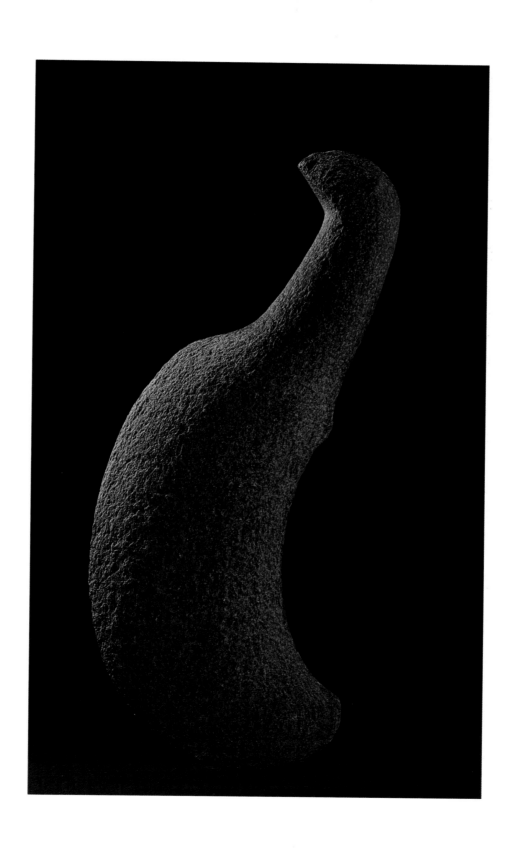

This archaic breast pendant from Okains Bay, Banks Peninsula, South Island, dates from c. 1100. It is a rendering in stone of the pearl-shell pendants of Polynesia. The hatched and crosshatched fish forms are unique.

PRECEDING PAGE: Bird-shaped *okewa* club from Waitangi in the Chatham Islands. The Moriori people of the Chathams, almost wiped out by Maori invaders in the nineteenth century, retained a variety of archaic culture long after it had disappeared from the mainland.

RIGHT: Frozen Hill, halfway between Lewis Pass and Culverden.

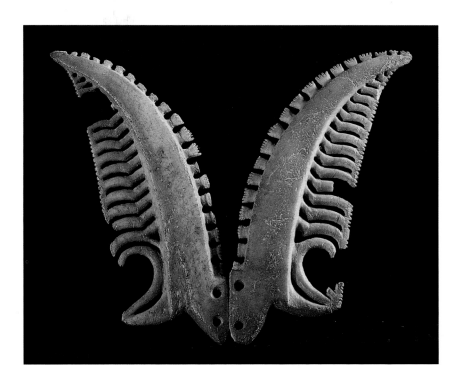

A pair of chevron pendants made of whale bone, from Kaikoura, north-eastern South Island.

LEFT: Arthur's Pass between Avalanche Peak and Falling Mountain, Southern Alps.

OVERLEAF: The next six photographs are of Pyramid Valley and Moa Swamp (near Waikari, North Canterbury) so named because of the bones of moas (giant flightless birds, now extinct) found in the swamp. Under the surface vegetation there is a layer of peat, and below that a calcareous jelly-like deposit, moist and oxygen free, formed when the site was a lake, and an ideal environment for the preservation of plant and animal remains. This area has been one of Forman's "finds". Why, he asks, has Moa Swamp, and also Claycliffs which follow (pp 192–194) not made it into the "scenic spots" league? "Although important and hauntingly beautiful," Forman remarks, "they remain almost unknown and – what a bonus! – unvisited. I spent at the height of the 1990 Commonwealth Games/Treaty Centenary carnival/celebrations razzle-dazzle, more than ten days in the isolation of Moa Swamp, from early new moon to full, eight/twelve/sixteen hours a day, and never a soul in sight."

Some of the photographs of this area, with dominant pinnacles seeming to stand forward of the landscape, have a typical Forman hologram effect; while pp 168–169 manage what one comes to think of as a characteristic Forman sky-and-cloud composition.

RIGHT: "Where the valley slopes down towards the east, forming a depression," notes Forman, "lies just discernible in the far background the Moa Swamp, a scientists' treasure-trove. Back in 1938 the present owner's grandfather faced a problem: to dispose of a dray horse's carcass on the land he owned was not going to be simple. Instead of cutting into one of the rocky hillsides, he chose to dig into the mud of a swamp, but getting rid of an unwanted possession turned out to be less straightforward than he had envisaged. Digging he brought to the surface three gigantic bones for which he, a farmer, had no better use than for his dead horse. Far from having solved his dilemma, it was growing in a perplexing fashion. Wisely, he sought expert help. The identification of the hefty triple nuisance as the legbones of *Dinornis maximus*, the biggest moa to have lived in Australasia over millions of years, made the swamp a focus of exploration. Besides other finds, 50 complete moas were recovered. An egg, still unlaid, found within one of the birds caused quite a stir. The overall yield goes beyond the obvious, the preservation of the remains, allowing a reconstruction of the past not to be surpassed by any Jurassic Park's make-believe drama."

OVERLEAF: Leaving Pyramid Valley, sunset.

Barry Lynch, born in Christchurch, makes a living as a punter on the Avon River.

OPPOSITE: Old boat-houses on the Avon River which ambles through Christchurch parks and gardens, willow stems trailing in its calm waters, helping probably more than any other single feature to give Christchurch its reputation for being the most English city outside of England.

This fire engine saw "active service" in Christchurch from 1915 to 1948. Forman records that the engine had to be cranked to start, that its lanterns were "match-lit", that it carried "a few bucketfuls" of water in its "wardrobe-shaped superstructure", that its one ladder fully extended "reached most second-floor sills", and that its greatest impact at any calamity must have been on the psyche of bystanders. A fireman of those years would no doubt disagree. But its era closed with Christchurch's great Ballantyne's department store fire of 1947 in which more than 50 people died.

Alf's Imperial Army, began in Melbourne, passed through Auckland, and has come to rest in Christchurch, an appropriate home for it. It is committed to pacifist war, mainly against all forms of authority, pomposity, bureaucracy, and humourlessness.

This branding iron (for sheep) in the form of a candlestick was registered at Christ-church by Samuel Butler in November 1860. After graduating from Cambridge, Butler came to New Zealand to improve his fortune. He established his sheep run of about 2000 hectares, which he called "Mesopotamia" (the name still used), on the upper reaches of the Rangitata River, below the Southern Alps. Butler's most notable work, *Erewhon*, before it moves into its satiric fantasy world, draws upon his experiences in New Zealand. His letters to his father were published as *First Year in a Canterbury Settlement*.

RIGHT: Mill Cottage, Greham Valley, Akaroa, on Banks Peninsula, 82 km by road, 40 as the crow flies, from Christchurch. French settlers arrived in Akaroa in 1840 only to find that the South Island had been annexed by the British. Some stayed, however, and many French names and elements remain. The Mill was built of pit-sawn *totara* in 1852 by Charles Haylock and his four sons, shortly after the Haylock family had survived seven terrible months at sea getting to New Zealand. They set up the first flour mill in the Canterbury region and operated it for a number of years.

A ring of sheltering hills encloses the safe harbour of Akaroa at the heart of Banks Peninsula, which juts out into the unpredictable South Pacific. Visible on the shore in the background is Akaroa township. On the right, jutting out into the harbour bay, is Onawe Peninsula.

The landscape as a human breast: looking across Akaroa Harbour from Le Bons Bay towards Duvauchelle and the west of Banks Peninsula, after sunset.

Evening, Banks Peninsula.

RIGHT: Mt Cook from the north, with Tasman Glacier below, following the line of the foothills.

In Maori legend, where so much happens on a Wagnerian scale, it is said the glaciers are frozen tears of a young woman whose lover, following her on a climb to the summit, fell and was killed. The gods were moved by her weeping, and preserved her tears as a memorial to her love.

PRECEDING PAGE: This is commonly the view of Mt Cook, New Zealand's highest peak (3764 m), which tourists come from all around the world to see. It is taken from the Hermitage hotel. The mountain's shifting veils of cloud are extremely unpredictable, and a sighting can never be guaranteed. Sometimes the peak vanishes for days at a time, and the reappearance is all the more astonishing. Sometimes it appears and disappears in a moment, glinting white in sunlight when the visitor's back is turned, or the photographer is putting in a new film.

The mountain was named, of course, after the navigator Captain James Cook (1720–79), who in 1769 made the second European discovery of New Zealand (Abel Tasman's, in 1642, was the first). Cook made the first, and still very good, maps of both islands, and gave European names to many of the bays, harbours and headlands.

The Maori name for the mountain is Aorangi or Aoraki according to the local people, the Kai Tahu.

Flight over Mt Cook. The Southern Alps run for six or seven hundred kilometres down most of the western side of the South Island and, together with the three major peaks in the North Island, Ruapehu, Tongariro and Ngaruahoe, have provided the training ground for New Zealand's best-known mountaineers, including Sir Edmund Hillary, and competitive skiers. Scores of peaks exceed 2000 metres, and seventeen rise above 3000. Mt Cook (3764 m) was first climbed in 1894, since when many have reached its summit, and more than a few have died in the attempt.

OPPOSITE: For Werner Forman, whose fascination with aeroplanes preceded, and led to, his profession as a photographer, the Southern Alps were clearly a subject to be treated from the air. Here he looks down on Mt Cook from (he notes) "as high as Cessna and photographer could climb without oxygen, and less one door to give the photographer an uncluttered view".

OVERLEAF: Hall Range.

Stars over Mt Cook, Hooker River Valley and Mt Wakefield.

OPPOSITE: Mt Cook (3764 m) and to its right Mt Tasman (3497 m) seen from the air, the last of the evening light still reaching the peaks but gone from the valleys and glacial river beds.

OVERLEAF: A last look back at Mt Cook across Lake Pukaki (with a Forman feather-cloud signature for effect!).

Claycliffs near Omarama in the central South Island is (like Pyramid Valley and Moa Swamp) another Forman "find", a place which he points out has been unaccountably neglected by the tourist industry and by photographers. (The owners of Claycliffs complain that stills taken by a Japanese TV crew gave the impression of diminutive fuzzy sandcastles.) The Claycliffs area is a spectacular example of what is called "badland" erosion – tall sharp bare pinnacles and ridges separated by deep ravines and canyons, formed when a suitable rock, in this case compacted gravel and silt, is eroded by a climate of sluicing watercourses and sudden heavy rainstorms. See also the caption for the title page (on p 4), where Forman reflects on the innapropriate term "Badlands" applied to this monumental landscape.

RIGHT: Evidence suggests that the natural fortification of Omarama was sporadically used as a retreat by early Maori people at the time when moas were still alive. Why the inhabitants of the chalk cliffs left remains unexplained.

Sun and cloud at Claycliffs.

Back to the coast in an exalted mood: St Mary's Anglican Church, Timaru. (See text p 14 for a discussion of this photograph).

Rain forest south of Mt Kinnon Pass, Fiordland. The Pass takes trampers on the famous Milford Track over a high saddle (1036 m) between the valleys of the Clinton and Arthur rivers. Noting that this forest, "every inch of it covered by a symbiotic green carpet, borders on glacial rivers, snow-bound mountains and stony, barren plateaux", Forman remarks, "environmental variations on the islands of New Zealand are astonishing".

This "upside down meadow drying under a hot tin roof", Forman says, might suggest "Antipodean ikebana". He adds that it is more of a "green" indulgence by the owners of Three Spring Station than a reliable or serious source of supplementary income.

Just north of Katiki Beach is Moeraki Point with its famous boulders, natural stone concretions measuring up to 3 m in circumference and weighing several tonnes. Maori legend has it that the ancestral canoe, Arai-te-uru, was wrecked here, and became the long reef that can be seen offshore at Shag Point, the southern end of Katiki Beach. The boulders are calabashes and food baskets lost overboard. A prominent rock is the navigator, and the chief and his crew form the coastal range. If Maui could fish up the whole of the North Island, these sizes don't seem in the least out of scale.

Of this photograph of the Moeraki boulders, taken almost ten years after the three shots on the preceding pages, Forman says: "In this repeat I attempt to show some of the moods of this coast relevant to the Maori legend, the point of departure lost in time and space, the crossing and landfall, the wreck and the spilling of the *kumara*-Moerakis."

Moorhouse Railway Station's signal box. The track Ferrymead to Moorhouse is part of the oldest railway in New Zealand.

OPPOSITE: An approaching train with its headlamp alight appears in this detail of a stained glass window in Dunedin Railway station.

Antiquated railway stock, Dunedin, dating from the 1870s.

Dunedin Railway Station, built, 1903–7, of stone quarried in Central Otago, is the city's fourth, a classic Victorian-style station that would have been appreciated by John Betjeman. Red Peterhead granite from Aberdeen, Scotland, and white Oamaru stone, have been used for ornamentation. The mosaics in the main foyer depict phases of railway work. They contain 725,760 squares of porcelain (c. 1.25 x 1.25 cm).

ABOVE LEFT: *Moko* (facial tattoo) pattern of Tuhawaiki, chief of the Kai Tahu, Otago, used as his signature on a deed of sale of land in the Catlins, January 1840. Now in the Hocken Library, University of Otago.

ABOVE RIGHT: Pakeha signature and self-portrait of the architect Edward Ramsay.

OPPOSITE: Rangi the sky father and Papa the earth mother locked in the perpetual embrace from which they were separated only by the efforts of Tane, god of the forests. (See Introduction p 15 for this myth.) Representing the gods as a copulating couple, this carving (from the entrance to a *pataka* or storehouse) held in the Otago Museum might be seen as a Maori challenge to the southern Scots, famous like their forefathers for Presbyterian puritanism with (alcohol-assisted) outbreaks of sin. Traditional Maori carving was often sexually explicit, causing our founding fathers and mothers confusion and concern. For a time the figures became neuter (or were neutered), but in the recent revival of Maori carving explicit genitalia are returning. Apirana Taylor has a short story about a young Maori carver who is asked to do a cross for a church. He mixes Maori and Christian symbolism, including the *tara* (female genitalia) of Hine-nui-te-po, the death goddess, as part of the decoration, causing shock and displeasure.

Matthew Thompson, 20 years old, student in Dunedin Art School's Prints and Ceramics Department.

Frances Baskerville, aged six. A study in concentration – *un peu vif, un peu doux, très grave*.

OVERLEAF: Queenstown and the Remarkables catching the last light after sundown. How Forman has kept both foreground interiors and distant mountains simultaneously in focus will perhaps not be a mystery to professional photographers, as it is to the author of this text; but the effect is certainly mysterious, catching as it does something of that contrast, so sharp and ever-present in New Zealand, between the domestic, the orderly, the very nearly banal on the one hand, and on the other the wild, the unregulated, the untameable.

Queenstown, with its "gondola" (cable car up the mountain) for viewing Lake Wakatipu and the mountains, is one of the most charming and popular of the South Island's tourist resorts.

After first operating out of a tent, the Colonial Bank (later the Bank of New Zealand) in Arrowtown opened in a wooden weatherboard building. Later it moved to "a bombastic building, completely out of tune with the surrounding simple architecture" (Forman's description), and then abandoned that for use as a museum and moved back to the original premises. Through the mining period $12 million worth of gold was handled by this bank. One of the rare photographs in which Forman has allowed so much as his shadow to be caught in the frame!

OPPOSITE: House and garden in old Queenstown. The standing stump and the overgrown vegetable garden evoke late colonial New Zealand.

Horse with matching stone stable, which was originally a dwelling built in Orkney style in 1864 by James Reid from Stromness, Orkney mainland, two years after gold was discovered in what became Arrowtown. His grandson, Jack Reid, owns the property.

The twentieth century caught in a shaft of light between Queenstown and Kingston.

In this detail of a *pataka* panel (see p 105) the fine craftsmanship is evident and one can see clearly how the fluid forms are made up of snake-like intertwining elements, creating a tension that seems at once creative and destructive. Within the broad and expansive outlines of each head, the inner features describe straight lines tapering directly up the high-domed conical foreheads. The ridges of pattern, extraordinarily bold and deeply carved, vary from unadorned to intricate notching, decorated in places with radiating lines.

PRECEDING PAGES: Milford Sound. This 15 km, narrow canyon-like opening to the sea is a true fiord – a glacial trough cut through 1800 m mountains which rise on either side, and deeper in its inner reaches (290 m) than at its entrance, the sea having flowed over a rock barrier and into it as the glacial ice receded. Rivers which were once tributary glaciers cascade into the Sound sometimes down 1200 m vertical walls of rock.

OPPOSITE: The upper Taieri River (seen from the air) meanders over a flatland cut by diluvial glaciers pushing huge masses of ice towards the coast. The convoluted pattern is the permanent riverbed, unchanged by recent flooding.

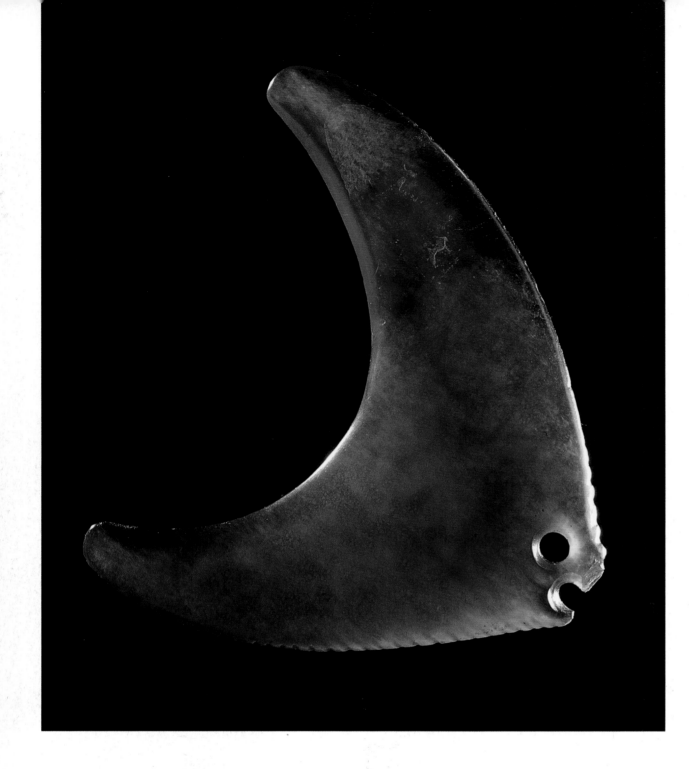

LEFT: One of the most beautiful Maori amulets made from semi-translucent bowenite in the form of a fish (7.3 cm high). Found at Otaga Heads, Ruapuke Island, South Island.

BELOW: A pair of fish-hook-shaped *hei matau* (amulets) of nephrite, from Banks Peninsula. The one on the right comes from the Southland area. A deliberate "mouth" has been made below the eye to represent an upraised seal – the hook is the tail. The one on the left was found while road-making in the Paekakariki area, Wellington, and is similar to Banks Peninsula examples.

OPPOSITE: Forman writes: "Maori legends tell of volcanoes belching red-hot violence, of heroes and of giants fishing islands out of the sea. Different in mood is this close-up of mushrooms in a green woodland scene, evocative of the fairy tales of northern Europe – a court of dwarfs, perhaps, somehere in the Black Forest." The location is Burnt City, Rotorua.

222

Forman's note reads: "By far the most typical Maori fence – some wood, but mostly imps."